Biblical Christian Fundamentals

Tomas Ramirez III

TRILOGY CHRISTIAN PUBLISHERS
TUSTIN, CA

Trilogy Christian Publishers
A Wholly Owned Subsidiary of Trinity Broadcasting Network
2442 Michelle Drive
Tustin, CA 92780

Biblical Christian Fundamentals

For information about special discounts for bulk purchases, please contact Trilogy Christian Publishing.

Manufactured in the United States of America

10 9 8 7 6 5 4 3 2 1

Library of Congress Cataloging-in-Publication Data is available.

ISBN: 978-1-63769-388-9

E-ISBN: 978-1-63769-389-6

Thank You

The idea for this book came to me approximately ten years ago, but a hectic schedule at work and at home kept me from ever making the time to commence and complete the project. For years, I shrugged off the idea of writing this book until I finally gave in to the calling and made time, mostly on Sundays, to write. After completing my initial draft, I asked for a few friends to read the draft and provide me critique and insight. I am most grateful to Dr. David Cooke, Richard Cottle, Ken Bowyer, Dr. Steve Spivey, and Linda McAnelly for their efforts. Each took the time to read the draft and provide me valuable comments, insights, and suggestions. I took what each provided and tried to incorporate it into the final version, which is what you have before you. I am so thankful that God provides wisdom and direction through other believers who are willing to give of their own time and talents to further the kingdom of God.

I would also like to give a special thanks to my wife, Dee Dee. She was the one who kept encouraging me to write this book because, she said, it could have a lasting and meaningful effect on those who read it, all to the glory of God. Her gentle reminders and nudging helped move me off the couch and onto my computer. Honey, you have truly enriched my life, and I am better off for having you in it! I love you very much.

The Purpose of This Book

For many years growing up and even into adulthood, I often wondered why so many different people gave so many different answers to questions pertaining to God and heaven and sin and lots of other topics that centered around my religious beliefs. How could things that should have been readily known and consistent across people of faith be so varied from person to person? Could it be that people had become so ignorant to the fundamental truths regarding God that there was no consistency in their beliefs?

One thing I knew was certain was that all of these people with varied ideas regarded the Bible as authoritative. I thought, *But how could this be? Surely God cannot be round, square, and shapeless all at the same time. The God who created the universe and the laws that govern it must be a God of order and logic.* After further inquiry, it became clear that even though these people regarded the Bible as a direct revelation from God, very few knew much about it at all! They had formed their beliefs from information they had received from another person, from their own personal experiences, or simply from what they felt was right. I was amazed and stunned (although I shouldn't have been).

In truth, I had been just as they were. But in 1996, while struggling with all of these varied ideas about God, I went to God in prayer and in much frustration. I told God that I knew there could only be one truth about God and that I didn't know what that truth was. I reminded God that because of His blessings to me, I had always excelled academically. I told God that I would study the Bible from cover to cover if He would teach me as I studied. I would study with absolutely no preconceived ideas such as: "Was there a heaven?" I don't know. "Is Jesus God?" I don't know, etc. I had been very successful in my life, and I told God that I wanted to know the Bible better than I knew anything. I would start with a set of notecards and would make categories for different topics, such as Characteristics of God, Sin, Deity of Jesus, etc. Anytime I would read a passage that fell under one of these categories, I would note the concept and the location in scripture. Little did I know that when Jesus said, *"And I say unto you, Ask, and it shall be given you; seek, and ye shall find; knock, and it shall be opened unto you"* (Luke 11:9), He was serious! It took me over two years to progress through the entire Bible, but when I finished, I could clearly see what had always been blurry. By no means, however, was I now a Bible scholar! I only had a set of clear lines that outlined basic and fundamental truths about God, but there was still very much to learn. I have been studying the Bible daily ever since, and I am still learning. I have come to conclude that in this life, no man can ever plumb the depths of God's Holy Bible, though we must continue trying.

There are certain fundamental truths that all believers must understand, for God has called us all to study His word so that we may know it and be ready to give an account to others when opportunities arise. This book is intended for new believers, for older Christians who are still "babes in Christ," for seekers who have never understood the basics of the Christian faith, and for anybody else wanting to know more about the Bible. But this book is also designed to show an unbeliever the grace and mercy of God, which He displayed in full glory through Jesus Christ. This book's purpose is to provide clear teaching as to the basic doctrines of the Christian faith according to what God has laid out in the Bible, which is often in sharp contrast to what we have learned elsewhere. Each chapter will cover a different subject, or a different aspect of a subject, that I consider basic. If this book were a college class, it would be called *Biblical Christianity 101*. It will cover subjects such as Jesus' death, prayer, our sin nature, whether the

Bible supports the doctrine of the Trinity and others. Every chapter deals with something foundational that every Christian should clearly understand.

It is my hope and prayer that God will take this book and use it to the glory of His name, for the advancement of His kingdom, for the enlightenment of the lost, and for the edification of His saints.

Tomas "Tommy" Ramirez III
August 30, 2020

Contents

CHAPTER 1

Salvation: the Work of God, Man, or Both?

You've surely heard the old saying, "If it sounds too good to be true, it probably is," or what about, "There is nothing free in this world." I have my own: "Everything free has a price." We have all seen offers where you buy one and get one free. I once went to a local hamburger restaurant chain offering such a promotion and told the person taking my order that I didn't want the first hamburger; I only wanted the second (free) one. After the puzzled look on her face disappeared, she promptly took my money as I paid for the burgers. That second burger really wasn't free; I just paid half price for two burgers.

When it comes to the salvation of a human soul where the ultimate destination is an eternity with God in heaven (or an eternity away from God in hell), most of us are convinced that we must earn it and our good deeds must outweigh the bad; after all, nothing is free. But is that what the Bible teaches? You might be surprised to find that the answer is a clear NO.

When speaking to the Jewish religious leader, a man named Nicodemus, Jesus surprised this respected teacher by saying, *"Verily, verily, I say unto thee, Except a man be born again, he cannot see the kingdom of God"* (John 3:3). In other words, unless a person becomes born again, he cannot go to heaven. Nicodemus was befuddled and responded by asking, "How can a man be born when he is old? Can he enter the second time into his mother's womb and be born again?" Jesus, in turn, responded, *"That which is born of the flesh is flesh; and that which is born of the Spirit is spirit"* (John 3:6). Jesus brought up a concept that Nicodemus had never considered; that is, that there is a difference between the birth of the body and the birth of the spirit. Never had it crossed the mind of Nicodemus that there could be the birth of the spirit; he had always equated the two in the single act of childbirth. Jesus drew a distinction between them, and it startled this man.

What is "born again"? You must understand that when Adam sinned in the Garden of Eden, he became a sinner and was "dead" to God. They could no longer walk together and spend time together as they did before the fall. All men born from this point forward were born after the nature of Adam and were born into death. Paul put it this way: *"Wherefore, as by one man [Adam] sin entered into the world, and death by sin; and so death passed upon all men, for that all have sinned"* (Romans 5:12) *(brackets added for clarity)*. So all of us are born through the flesh after the nature of Adam, and we are all born into death. Jesus said we need to have a second birth in order to live before God, and that second birth consists of not being born after the nature of Adam and the flesh but being born by the Spirit of God through faith; new life created inside of us after *God's* nature, not man's. This is the second birth, and it can only happen by God's grace.

Throughout the Bible, the same message emerges over and over again: salvation is the work of God provided freely to man and triggered by man's faith; salvation is the result of God's grace. Before proceeding any further, we must define grace. According to Webster's dictionary (1828 edition), grace is "the free, unmerited love and favor of God." Notice the key portion of this definition: it is "unmerited," that is, it is not something that is earned or deserved. This is exactly what the Bible teaches. For example:

> For if Abraham were justified by works, he hath whereof to glory; but not before God. For what saith the scripture? Abraham be-

lieved God, and it was counted unto him for righteousness. Now to him that worketh is the reward not reckoned of grace, but of debt. But to him that worketh not, but believeth on him that justifieth the ungodly, his faith is counted for righteousness.

Romans 4:2-5

Here we see that the apostle Paul reminds us that Abraham did not obtain his salvation by anything he did (his works) because if he had to work for it, then it would have been a debt God owed to him. The payment of this debt would have negated grace. Paul ends this section of scripture by reminding the reader that the person who doesn't try to earn salvation but just believes that faith is counted to that individual as righteousness before God. Later in *Romans*, Paul writes it this way: *"For the wages of sin is death; but the gift of God is eternal life through Jesus Christ our Lord" (Romans 6:23).* Do you see it? Salvation (eternal life) is a gift. We all know that a gift is something you receive for absolutely nothing; you don't do anything for it, and you don't pay anything for it. If you have to do something or pay some price to receive the gift, then it is no longer a gift but something you bought or earned.

In Ephesians 2:8-9, Paul writes: *"For by grace are ye saved through faith; and that not of yourselves: it is the gift of God: not of works, lest any man should boast."* Let's break down this verse because it is packed with information. First, notice that we are saved by grace; that is the same thing Paul wrote in the *Romans 4* passage above. It is God's grace that reaches out to save the human soul. If God didn't reach out with His grace, no human soul would, or could, be saved. Let me give you an illustration. I grew up in deep south Texas in a very rural area where cattle was a major industry. I saw spiders of all sorts from the time I was very young. I watched in fascination mixed with horror as flies, grasshoppers, and other insects got caught in the spider's web. It didn't take me very long to realize that once the insect was in the web, it could not escape. Its fate was sealed, and nothing the insect could do would ever free it from the web and certain death. One day when I was a teenager, I happened upon a grasshopper that had leaped into the web of a spider. Before the spider could descend upon the insect to inject its deadly venom, I took a stick and pulled the grasshopper out of the web. The grasshopper escaped certain death that day. Now, what did the grasshopper do to escape death and "earn" his freedom? Absolutely nothing. It was pure grace on my part. If I had not intervened, the grasshopper would have surely died (right before my eyes). Salvation with God is exactly the same. God looked upon the fallen condition of man and saw that man had no way to escape the certain death that the web of sin demanded unless He personally intervened. (See *Romans 5:8.*) Horatio G. Spafford, who wrote the famous hymn *It is Well With My Soul*, captured this truth so well when he wrote, "Christ has regarded my helpless estate and has shed His own blood for my soul." So we can now better understand Paul's statement that we are saved by God's grace.

Next thing we see in the *Ephesians* passage is the mechanism by which God has chosen to save us: faith. We are saved by grace through faith. God has decreed that the soul who will be saved must have faith. Now having faith is a pretty vague statement, and if that was the only passage in the Bible on the subject, we would have a hard time understanding what this means. I remember telling my grandmother about Jesus and his cross and resurrection many years ago. She looked at me, and, as sincerely as she could, she told me that it didn't matter what I believed, just as long as I really believed it. She said God would be fine with that. I responded, pointing to the white brick on our house, and asked her: "So if you really and truly believe this brick can save you, that is good enough with God?" She just smiled and had no response. But the Bible is clear on this matter too. Jesus said: *"For God so loved the world, that he gave his only begotten Son, that whosoever believeth in him should not perish, but have everlasting life"* (John 3:16). John the Baptist put it this way: *"He that believeth on the*

Son hath everlasting life: and he that believeth not the Son shall not see life; but the wrath of God abideth on him" (John 3:36). So from these two passages alone, we see that God makes it clear where our faith must lie: it must be in Jesus. This is exactly how we are born again!

"But it can't be that easy," you may say. "The devil believes in Jesus, and he isn't saved. After all, he talked to Jesus when he tempted Him in the wilderness. There has to be more to it." Our faith is focused on the work of Jesus on the cross and his resurrection from the dead; that this is sufficient to save a human soul. Paul writes again:

> For it pleased the Father that in him [Jesus] should all fullness dwell; and, having made peace through the blood of his cross, by him to reconcile all things unto himself; by him, I say, whether they be things in earth, or things in heaven. And you, that were sometime alienated and enemies in your mind by wicked works, yet now hath he reconciled in the body of his flesh through death, to present you holy and unblameable and unreproveable in his sight.
>
> *Colossians 1:19-22*
> (brackets added for clarity)

Here Paul reminds us that Jesus made peace for us through His blood on the cross. The passage goes on to state that He took sinners who were alienated and lost and reconciled us in His body through His death. This is the focus of the saved person's faith, along with Jesus' resurrection. The devil has never believed that Jesus died for him, nor will he ever.

Paul also states in *Romans 10:9*, *"That if thou shalt confess with the mouth the Lord Jesus, and shalt believe in thine heart that God hath raised him from the dead, thou shalt be saved."* Here we see the resurrection aspect of our faith. Paul wrote to the Corinthian church that if God never raised Jesus from the dead, our faith is vain, and we are still lost in our sins (*1 Corinthians 15:16-17*).

Now back to the *Ephesians* passage. We see that we are saved by God's grace and that God's vehicle to obtain salvation is faith in Jesus' death and resurrection. Paul continues the passage by writing, "and that not of yourselves; it is the gift of God; not of works lest any man should boast." The *"that"* in this sentence used to always confuse me, as I never understood why it was there. I have come to understand that the *"that"* refers to our salvation ("For by grace ye are saved through faith") in the previous portion of the passage. So the passage could read: "and your salvation is not of yourselves..." Paul is emphasizing that the salvation of the human soul is not of our own doing; it is simply a gift that God has provided to us (and he says so consistently, such as in *Romans 5:15*). Then he reminds us once again that it is not of works, lest any man should boast. If this were not the case, and we all had to "earn" our way to heaven, then can you imagine the conversations amongst the saved once we get there?

Pedro: "Hey Joe, how did you get here (to heaven)?"

Joe: "Well, I visited orphans for twenty years and donated tens of thousands of dollars to their orphanage."

Pedro: "That's nothing. I traveled for twenty-five years across the ocean to work among the pygmies in Africa. We didn't even have running water or electricity."

On and on, the comparisons and boastings would echo through God's glorious heaven. There is no love in boasting, only pride. God has stated that salvation is not the function of man's endeavors, or donations, or prayers, or church attendance, or service to our fellow-man, or any other work. If it were, then man would have lots of room to boast. But God says there is no boasting because everybody's answer to Pedro's question will be exactly the same: "Jesus died for my sins and washed me clean through His blood." Salvation is purely the gracious work of God.

CHAPTER 2

Was Man Born with Original Sin or Merely with the Tendency to Sin?

So here is a question for you: "Do we sin because we are sinners, or are we sinners because we have sinned?" The answer provides insight into the essence of our nature before God. Before we address the question, however, we should define "sin" so that we are all clear on its meaning. The Merriam-Webster dictionary defines sin as "transgression of the law of God; an offense against religious or moral law; a vitiated state of human nature in which the self is estranged from God." Sin, then, is violating God's laws and standards which He has established, and we are all guilty of it. (See Chapter, *How to be Saved*.) But, according to Webster, it is also our human state that is estranged (or separated) from God. The result of our sinful nature is being separated from God. Now let us examine the question posed above.

The Newborn Baby

It is difficult to imagine that an innocent newborn baby can be a sinner. After all, the infant has no concept of life, no knowledge of the world or its Creator, cannot comprehend anything but the most basic of emotional urges, and certainly does not know the difference between right and wrong as defined by God. The child is helpless, harmless, and totally dependent on some person, usually a parent, for his continued survival. Many would argue that the child is "innocent" and is not yet capable of sin. Do you agree? The Bible says that this newborn child is already a sinner. *"The wicked are estranged from the womb: they go astray as soon as they be born, speaking lies"* (Psalm 58:3). According to the psalmist, the newborn baby is already sinning at birth! The child cannot utter a single word, yet the Bible says he is speaking lies as soon as he is born. This statement seems inconceivable from a human understanding. After all, our experience tells us a child cannot speak anything, truth or lies. However, man cannot see the human heart as God can. Jeremiah stated that the human heart is deceitful above all things and desperately wicked (Jeremiah 17:9), and it is the human heart with which every man is born that is his downfall. Jesus said the heart is the place where sin originates within man (*Matthew 12:35*). This explains the reason that a man must be "born again," as Jesus stated to Nicodemus in John 3. A new nature must be born from above, which will co-exist with the old, sinful nature inherent in our bodies. *The old nature that we are born with does not become corrupt because we sin, instead we sin because the old nature we are born with is already corrupt.* Because of this, all believers must be born again.

Still, some may argue the psalmist is not stating that the child is born a sinner. These argue that the child is not a sinner at birth but that he is born pure and merely sins immediately after birth. This is not supported by the Bible; notice the first part of the verse, "The wicked are estranged from the womb..." To be estranged is to be separated. Estranged from what? That is the question that immediately presents itself. The answer is simple, estranged from God, just as we read in the Merriam-Webster definition. God cannot have fellowship with a sinner until his sins are forgiven through faith in Jesus Christ. According to the Bible, it is from the womb that we are all estranged. "Wait a minute!" you may be saying. "It says 'the wicked' are estranged from the womb. It doesn't mention the righteous. You are lumping all of humanity into this verse, and that is not accurate." But it is accurate. The Bible is quite clear, *"There is none righteous, no, not one" (Romans 3:10).* "But that is true because everybody eventually sins. That is not necessarily true for everybody at birth." Hold on. It will become clearer.

David, I believe, knew the truth about this matter when he stated, *"Behold, I was shapen in iniquity; and in sin did my mother conceive me" (Psalm 51:5)*. Here, David is stating that while he was being formed within the womb, sin had already infected him. Notice also the last part of the verse, "in sin did my mother conceive me." Does this mean that David's mother was sinning when she conceived him? Of course not. There is no sin in having sexual relations with your spouse *(Hebrews 13:4)*. David is stating that from the moment of his conception, the first moment of life, he was already contaminated with sin. His mother conceived him not in purity but in sin. Notice what Isaiah the prophet had to say:

> Yea, thou heardest not; yea, thou knewest not; yea, from that time that thine ear was not opened: for I knew that thou wouldest deal very treacherously, and wast called a transgressor from the womb.
>
> *Isaiah 48:8* (emphasis added)

What is sin? Sin is a transgression against God. Isaiah makes it clear that from the womb, a person is a transgressor against the Almighty. God calls us transgressors from the time we are in the womb before physical birth. As such, all mankind is born a sinner before any action has ever been taken.

Virgin Birth of Jesus

Isaiah 7:14 prophesied that a virgin would give birth to God. The Gospels of *Luke* and *Matthew* confirm the fact that Mary was a virgin when the Holy Spirit came upon her and life sprang up in her womb. Why was a virgin birth necessary? Was God doing something simply to show the world that this child was to be special, or was there a deeper meaning to this act? In order to comprehend this truth, one must understand that Jesus was born for one reason and one reason only...to die for the sins of mankind on the Roman cross at Calvary as had been prophesied by the Old Testament prophets years before. *"Even as the Son of man came not to be ministered unto, but to minister, and to give his life a ransom for many"* (Matthew 20:28).

God laid out the rules and requirements for dealing with sin in the Old Testament. He provided that blood had to be shed to address sin, and the manner for these sacrifices was recorded in the Bible by Moses. *Exodus 12:5* states the main criteria God established for the sacrificial lamb that would be slaughtered to atone for the sins of man; the lamb had to be without spot or blemish, i.e., sinless. (Remember that the animal sacrifices of the Old Testament were a picture or foreshadowing of the true Lamb that was to come. See *Hebrews 10*.) As such, Jesus Christ would have to be without spot or blemish in order for his sacrifice on the cross to be acceptable to God. *But had Jesus not been born to a virgin, then he could not have been sinless.*

> Wherefore, as by one man sin entered into the world, and death by sin; and so death passed upon all men, for that all have sinned...Nevertheless death reigned from Adam to Moses, even over them that had not sinned after the similitude of Adam's transgression, who is the figure of him that was to come.
>
> *Romans 5:12, 14*

It was absolutely necessary for Jesus not to be born from the line of Adam, else he would have been born a sinner, as outlined above. (Remember, a sinner can only beget a sinner.) For that reason, God Himself planted the seed in Mary's womb so that Jesus would not come from the sinful line of Adam but from the perfect, pure, and holy line of God. This is the reason that the doctrine of virgin birth is so important and why there is no room for compromise on this issue. For if Jesus was not virgin-born thus having an earthly father, then he was a sinner from the moment of his conception, having come from the sinful line of Adam; and as such, his sacrifice would have been in vain, and we would still be doomed to an eternity in hell. But give glory to God that Jesus was virgin-born, allowing Him to be born without sin, and further confirming that his sacrifice was totally acceptable to God as stated in *Isaiah 53:11*!

Jesus' Sacrifice Not Necessary If No Original Sin.

If mankind was not born with original sin, then I submit that it would not have been necessary for God to leave heaven's glory and come to suffer a humiliating death on the cross. After all, as we saw above, God's main criteria for the sacrificial lamb was that the lamb be sinless. Therefore, if mankind is not born a sinner, then he must be sinless at birth. As such, any one of the sinless male babies that have been born throughout the history of man could have been acceptable to God and offered as the sacrifice necessary to appease God's holy nature, thus saving mankind. You are probably thinking, "That is preposterous!" I agree; it is preposterous. Yet, one is forced to accept this notion if one maintains that all are born sinless with merely a tendency toward sin. We would simply have to offer the child as a sacrifice before he commits his first sin. (Nothing in the scriptures says the sacrificial lamb has to volunteer or has to be thirty-three years old or any other disqualifying criteria. Any sinless male person would be acceptable.) Still, I feel very confident that nobody would dare dispute that this is a ridiculous concept. It is ridiculous, however, *only because* not a single newborn baby in the history of mankind was born sinless. Jesus had to come down from heaven to become that sacrificial lamb because nobody else qualified!

It is this God-given knowledge of sin that allows us to worship and praise God for the wonderful, loving sacrifice that Jesus made on the cross and for His great grace. He took a doomed civilization of soiled sinners and gave them the opportunity to reside in His presence for all eternity. Praise the Lamb!

CHAPTER 3

The Futility of Religion: Can Any Religion Save?

How long have you been attending church or synagogue or prayer service or whatever religious gatherings that are normal to your life? Why do you attend? If we are honest, most of us attend church in order to gain favor with God so that we can ultimately go to heaven; it is what we are expected to do. Religion has been defined as "a particular system of faith and worship." But did you know that there is only one religion in the history of the world that God Himself actually created? Do you know what it is? Judaism. God personally created this religion and gave all of the instructions to Moses on Mount Sinai on how it was to be practiced. All other religions were created by man, some through their own wisdom and understanding, and some through alleged "supernatural intervention" (such as Mormonism or

Islam). But can any of these religions save a soul and yield eternal life with God? The answer, according to the Bible, is an absolute NO. So no matter what religion you have been practicing, the Bible is clear: not one of them is able to save anybody! Now, before you slam this book shut, refuse to consider it any longer, and label me an arrogant idiot, please read the rest of the chapter to allow me to explain what the Bible teaches on this very important subject.

After the Israelites left Egypt under the powerful hand of God, they were led through the wilderness to Mount Sinai, the mountain of God (see *Exodus 19*). While at Mount Sinai, God gave Moses the ten commandments and the law that would form the religion of the Jews, as seen in the books of *Exodus, Leviticus, Numbers,* and *Deuteronomy*. It has been said that this religion outlined over six hundred *dos* and *don'ts*, including the sacrificing of lambs, rams, goats, doves, and other animals for sin offerings, burnt offerings, peace offerings, and other such offerings. It required the keeping of feasts and holy days, a restriction of certain foods, the forbidding of certain acts, the requirement of others, and many other such things. God told Moses to tell the Jews,

> Ye shall do my judgments, and keep mine
> ordinances, to walk therein: I am the LORD

your God. Ye shall therefore keep my stat-
utes, and my judgments: which if a man do,
he shall live in them: I am the LORD.

Leviticus 18:4-5

So we can see that God Himself said that the people
were to obey His laws. The people believed, especially
as time went by, that in order to please God, they had
to obey. And if they obeyed, they would live. Thus, the
people began to believe that their salvation with God
was in their own hands...if they could do the things
God commanded, they would be fine; if not, then their
doom was their own fault. But was the law given by God
to Moses created for that purpose? Not according to the
Bible. "Wait a minute," you may be saying. "Then why
did God give the law at all if it wasn't for their salvation?" Patience, and God provides the answer for us, as
shown below.

Before God ever gave the law, was anybody ever
saved? Clearly, that answer is yes. Abraham, Noah, Job,
Enoch, and Abel are clearly identified as saved individuals in the Bible (see *Hebrews 11:1-19*), yet each lived long
before the law was ever revealed to man by God. How
were these individuals saved without any law available? According to *Hebrews 11*, they were saved because
they each had faith, and it is that faith that saved them.
"That's vague," you may be saying, "faith in what?" Re-

garding Abraham, the Bible declares: *"And he believed in the LORD; and he [God] counted it to him [Abraham] for righteousness"* (Genesis 15:6). Abraham believed everything God had told him, and the actions of his life demonstrated his faith. God then declared that Abraham's faith in God's word to him, as proved by his actions, was the sole basis for Abraham's salvation. The same is true for Noah and the others, as written in *Hebrews 11*. So it is without dispute that salvation was available to man before God ever gave the law. "So did the law provide another avenue by which a soul could be saved?" you may be asking. No, it did not.

The author of the book of *Hebrews* reminded his Jewish audience that God had given the law (the first covenant), but that He had promised through Jeremiah the prophet that:

> Behold, the days come, saith the LORD, that I will make a new covenant with the house of Israel, and with the house of Judah: Not according to the covenant that I made with their fathers in the day that I took them by the hand to bring them out of the land of Egypt; which my covenant they brake, although I was an husband unto them, saith the LORD: But this shall be the covenant that I will make with the house of Israel; After those days,

saith the LORD, I will put my law in their in-
ward parts, and write it in their hearts; and
will be their God, and they shall be my people.

Jeremiah 31:31-33

Then the author of *Hebrews* states, *"For if the first covenant had been faultless, then should no place have been sought for the second" (Hebrews 8:7).* Did you catch that? He states that if the law, which he calls the first covenant, had been sufficient to save a human soul, there would not have been a need for a second covenant, which God had promised through Jeremiah. But he went on to state that the law given by God was totally insufficient for the removal of sins and the saving of a soul.

For the law having a shadow of good things
to come, and not the very image of the things,
can never with those sacrifices which they offered year by year continually make the com-
ers thereunto perfect.

Hebrews 10:1

In other words, the worshippers who were following the law and making the sacrifices continually year after year could not be made "perfect" by doing so. He continued by reminding his audience that these sacrifices had to be offered continually, year after year because they could not remove sins. *"But in those sacrifices there is a remembrance again made of sins every year. For it is not possible that the blood of bulls and of goats should take away sins" (Hebrews 10:3-4).* Can it be any clearer than that? All of the sacrifices offered to God by the people could not remove their sins. God went on to state that He took no pleasure in the sacrificial offerings being made by the people under the law *(Hebrews 10:8; Isaiah 1:11-14).* If these sacrifices were able to bring souls to salvation, God should have been extremely pleased; but they could not, for they were incapable of removing the stain of sin.

Well, if the law created and instituted by God Himself is not able to take away sins, and God took no pleasure in the sacrifices offered under the law, then why did God bother creating it in the first place? The law was created for the sole purpose of educating the Jewish people that they had a sin problem that required blood and death to resolve. When describing the method for sacrificing, God lays out that the sinner who is making the offering shall slay the sacrificial animal, and afterward, the priests who are on duty shall then work with the blood and the animal as God prescribed. (See *Leviticus 1:2-5, 10-11; 3:1-2, 7-8, 12-13.*) This means that the person who has sinned will see up close and personal the animal dying that he has slain. He will know that this animal is dying because of his sin, and he will quickly learn that his sin has a consequence of bloodshed and death. This is the purpose of the law, as stated by the apostle Paul in the book of Galatians: *"Wherefore the law was our schoolmaster to bring us unto Christ, that we might be justified by faith"* *(Galatians 3:24)*. The law was our "schoolmaster," Paul said. That term brings to mind a classroom of students being provided instruction and learning on material they have yet to comprehend by someone who already knows the subject. When the schoolmaster finishes the course, and if the students were astute, attentive, and wise, the students would then have a solid grasp on the subject taught. The same is true of the law ordained by God through Moses. The law was that schoolmaster who fully comprehended the subject of sin, death, and salvation. The Jewish people who received the law were the students who did not understand the truth of sin, death, and salvation. After hearing and applying the law to their own lives, the people would eventually learn the truth that they were sinners whose sin required death to deal with their sin. The sacrifices would never end because the law continually demanded them due to their constant sin. This was God's whole purpose of establishing the law.

But if the sacrifices of the law cannot take away sins, what can? What hope does anybody have to be clean before God? God has a Lamb whose blood has a cleansing power that is able to take away all sins, but only God's

Lamb can do so; none other can. Jesus is God's Lamb. John the Baptist identified Jesus at the beginning of his ministry when he stated, *"Behold the lamb of God, which taketh away the sin of the world" (John 1:29)*. John understood that Jesus was born into this world two thousand years ago for one purpose, and that purpose was to die as God's Lamb. Jesus Himself knew He would die long before He was ever born into the world. Hebrews tells us that Jesus spoke to God the Father when He said, *"Sacrifice and offering thou wouldest not, but a body hast thou prepared me" (Hebrews 10:5)*. In this recorded conversation, Jesus was acknowledging two things: (1) that the sacrifices and offerings of the law were not sufficient to satisfy the requirements of a Holy God regarding the sin of man, and (2) that God had prepared a "body" for Him. Why would God have to prepare a body for Jesus? Because Jesus would have to leave heaven to become human, being confined to a human body, in order to sacrifice Himself to save the souls of men.

> And you, that were sometime alienated and enemies in your mind by wicked works, yet now hath he reconciled in the body of his flesh through death, to present you holy and unblameable and unreproveable in his sight.
>
> *Colossians 1:21-22*

Only Jesus' blood was sufficient to do this mighty work of reconciliation of the lost soul to God, and that is why He willingly went to the cross to shed His blood and die. This was the only way to break the chains of sin irrevocably bound to the human soul and bring it salvation. Jesus said, *"If the Son therefore shall make you free, ye shall be free indeed"* (John 8:36). Abraham and Noah and Enoch and countless others believed this, and they have eternal life. "Hold on again!" you say. "There you go making statements that don't make any sense! How could Abraham and Noah and other such people believe this about Jesus when Jesus didn't live and go to the cross until hundreds and hundreds of years after they had lived?" The saints who lived before Jesus had the word from God either through oral tradition or through the writings of the Old Testament. They heard about the coming Messiah and His future work. They believed what they heard and lived their lives accordingly, hoping for that glorious day when the Messiah would appear to fulfill the words on which they had pinned all their hopes. When speaking about Abraham in regards to this truth, Jesus said, *"Your father Abraham rejoiced to see my day: and he saw it, and was glad"* (John 8:56). You see, the death and resurrection of Jesus is the pivotal event in all of human history on which the soul of every person who has ever lived, or will live, rest. It is the one and only moment in time when the Godhead was taking the steps needed to save humanity from certain death, and it was happening on a hill outside of the city of Jerusalem while a badly wounded and naked man was dying on a cross, and hardly anybody understood it when it was happening. All persons who lived before Jesus looked forward to the day of that blessed event for their salvation, and every person who has lived since that time looked backward to that same blessed event for their salvation.

So, the law given to Moses cannot save any human soul, and it never could; it doesn't have that power, and it wasn't created for that purpose even though it was penned by God Almighty Himself. That being absolutely true, then how can anybody believe that his or her religion today is sufficient to save their soul so long as they follow the mandates of that particular religion? If God's personal religion cannot save, then it is absolutely certain neither can anybody else's. It is only through faith in what Jesus has already done that a person can be saved. There is no other way. *"Jesus saith unto him, I am the way, the truth, and the life: no man cometh unto the Father, but by me"* (John 14:6). *"But without faith it is impossible to please him [God]: for he that cometh to God must believe that he is, and that he is a rewarder of them that diligently seek him"* (Hebrews 11:6) *(brackets added for clarity)*. Leave your religion and come to Jesus; there is no other way.

CHAPTER 4

What is Truth?

An amazing confrontation was occurring in the judgment hall of the procurator of Jerusalem many years ago. [A procurator was an imperial governor of a Roman province.] On one side was a vicious and hard man who had little regard for human life and suffering. He had ordered many people to be killed, and he was not a man with whom one trifled. His name was Pontius Pilate. On the other side was a poor man with a very large group of followers. This man had done so many good works in the community that one writer said these good works could not be numbered. He was wiser than any who ever lived, and He had unlimited power at His disposal, yet you would never have known that by looking at Him. He was wearing tattered clothes and was severely beaten and bruised. His name was Jesus of Nazareth. Now Pilate was accustomed to having persons accused of crimes brought before him for judgment, and he was also accustomed to the accused pleading, crying, and denying the crimes (after all, the punishment for being found guilty would have been severe, sometimes to the point of death), so he was not prepared for what followed. When Jesus was brought before Pilate, He initially would not answer any of Pilate's questions, which amazed Pilate. Instead of groveling and denying and making excuses, He said nothing. After further questioning, Jesus finally spoke but not in the usual manner Pilate was accustomed to seeing. Jesus was already beaten and bruised, yet He spoke matter-of-factly and made plain statements about His kingdom. Jesus said,

> Thou sayest that I am a king. To this end was I born, and for this cause came I into the world, that I should bear witness unto the truth. Every one that is of the truth heareth my voice.
>
> *John 18:37*

Pilate immediately answered, "What is truth?"

That question continues to echo through the annals of human history, and ultimately, every person's answer to that question drives their eternal destiny. If you have ever had a deep discussion about religion and God, you surely have discovered that most religious people seem to have strong ideas and beliefs which may not line up with your own. How can we know who is right? For example, I have many relatives that insist that since they have been baptized and they have taken holy communion, they are saved. When I respond by telling them God does not save souls in that manner, they tell me I am wrong. So who is right? Can we ever really know (before we die and we all find out for certain after it is too late)?

All differences of opinion and belief really boil down to one thing: what is the source of truth upon which everybody is relying to bolster their opinions and beliefs? In the case of my relatives, generally, their source of truth is what they have been told by their priests, nuns, some other authority, or some other family members. For other people, it is their experiences. Some people have had such vivid dreams or other encounters that those experiences form the basis of their theology. For example, Dr. Mary Neal had a life-after-death experience where she says she saw heaven and heard amazing things while she was clinically dead from drowning. That experience was so vivid and strong that it forms the basis for her beliefs today, even though many of those beliefs are not aligned with the revelations in the Bible. What do you rely upon when declaring your beliefs today? This question is all-important.

So if one person disagrees with another person about a particular aspect of religion and both are equally sure they are right, and the other is wrong based upon their particular source of truth, can we ever know who is right, or are both equally right or wrong? If there is no absolute truth, no source that is anchored and immovable where everybody can go to discover *God's* truth, then the human race is left to float adrift on an ocean of swirling ideas and philosophies that will surely scatter humanity everywhere. Nobody would ever be able to know what is true since everybody's source of truth would be different. But a loving God cannot leave the human race to float adrift without providing a sure compass and a rock-solid anchor, and rest assured...He did not.

Jesus prayed for His people in *John 17* before moving towards His death in a passage known as the high priestly prayer. In that prayer to His Father, Jesus said, *"Sanctify them through thy truth: thy word is truth"* (*John 17:17*). Jesus says that God's word is truth, and He obviously believed it because He used it to fight off the devil during His temptation in the wilderness, He taught his followers from it, and He cited it throughout His ministry. When Jesus was asked about spiritual truth, He would answer by quoting the scriptures. In one instance, for example, He was asked about the resurrection to which He replied that the truth of the matter was contained within the scriptures, *"Jesus answered and said unto them, Ye do err, not knowing the scriptures, nor the power of God"* (*Matthew 22:29*). When Paul the apostle was teaching in his writings about spiritual truth, he would say, *"For what saith the scripture?"* (Romans 4:3), *and "Nevertheless what saith the scripture?"* (Galatians 4:30). When settling questions of religion, both Jesus and Paul always turned to the Bible.

God would never leave humanity to drift aimlessly on countless points of view and beliefs in the hopes that man stumbles across the path to salvation. God gave us everything we need when He left us His word which is contained in the Holy Bible. "Wait a minute," you may be saying, "who said the Holy Bible is God's word? Why can't it be the Koran or the Book of Mormon or the teachings of Buddha or some other religious text? Maybe even a combination of them." That is a great question, and it has an equally great answer. First, neither Jesus, nor the apostles, nor the prophets ever quoted or relied upon any other book to cite spiritual truth, except for those contained in the Holy Bible. Second, God cannot lie (*Titus* 1:2), and the teachings of the Bible are often in direct conflict with these other writings. Since a baseball cannot be both round and square at the same time, only one can be true. And since the books of the Holy Bible were those used by Jesus and the others, then those must be true. Third, when the Holy Bible was being compiled, the participants involved in that process spent much time in prayer and research, trying to determine which books to include and which to leave out from the Bible. Do you believe that during this process,

God was in heaven with his fingers crossed, pacing the heavenly throne room floor, sweating while He hoped these men got things right? Of course not. God was in perfect and complete control of the outcome of that process. After all, God says that He will forever preserve His word (*Psalm 12:6-7*) because His word is necessary for the faith of a human soul (*Romans 10:17*). So we can be certain that the Holy Bible is exactly what it claims to be; the truth directly from the mouth of God.

"Okay, but how do I know that the Bible today is the same as it was when it came from God initially through His writers? There have been many centuries that have since passed, and I believe it's pretty safe to say that the 'truth' as revealed by God so long ago has been slowly but surely lost in translation." Again, please never forget that God promised that He will forever preserve His word! He has said it will never be lost. Now those very first, original manuscripts upon which Moses, Daniel, and Paul wrote are gone. Time has eroded those scrolls away, but we are certain that those original manuscripts were copied meticulously and carefully from the time they were written. Jewish scribes would work tirelessly and diligently to copy each manuscript exactly as it was originally written. These scribes had rules to follow during the copying process, and they were very detailed. For example, after a single page was copied (all by hand, of course, since copy machines did not exist until only very recently in human history), the scribe would count every letter on each line to make sure it matched the original; if the count was off at all, they would destroy the page and start over. They were very, very careful about every single detail because they held the words from God in the highest esteem. When the Dead Sea Scrolls were discovered in the 1940s, they were an archeological treasure. Those scrolls contained all the books of the Old Testament Bible (except for *Esther* and *Nehemiah*), and they were dated to about two hundred years before the birth of Jesus; that is a long time ago! A study of those old texts by biblical scholars has proved (to no surprise to the true believer) that our good Bible translations today are exactly the same! Just like God promised, He surely has preserved His word, and we can be absolutely confident that the Bible today is exactly as it was when God originally gave it to the prophets.

In the end, my source of truth is the Holy Bible because that was Jesus' source of truth, as well as the source for Paul and the other apostles and prophets. Why would anybody think they know better than these historical figures and choose to rely on some other book or even some experience? Some experiences are so vivid (such as Joseph Smith's [the founder of Mormonism] vision) that they are the dominant factor in their beliefs, surpassing the teachings of the Bible. And it is true that God has spoken in times past to His people in vivid visions. (For example, see 2 *Corinthians* 12:2-4.) But never has God contradicted Himself and voided portions of His written word through these visions. How can anybody be safe from false visions or false teachings if they don't know the Holy Bible? When the devil attacked Jesus in the wilderness, the devil quoted warped "truth." Jesus came back by skillfully handling the Holy Bible and corrected the contradiction or the lie. In the book of *The Revelation*, Jesus commends the church at Ephesus because *"thou hast tried them which say they are apostles, and are not, and hast found them liars"* (*Revelation* 2:2). How could they have "tried them"? By taking their teachings and comparing them with the revealed truth of God's word. That is exactly what we must do today. It is the only way to navigate through this world of spiritual deceit and decay.

"Is it necessary to actually read and study the Bible? Can't we just believe God and serve Him without reading it? After all, I never can understand it, and the whole process becomes a waste of time." In the chapter *Salvation: The Work of God, Man, or Both?* we discuss how a person is saved. But suffice it to say for now that without God's word, nobody can be saved. Now try to remember back to your first crush in grade school. The person you liked was just wonderful, and you wished you could spend lots of time being near that person and talking to him/her. You wanted to know everything you could about the person, such as his/her favorite color, birthday, hobbies, etc. You studied that person, noting how he/she styled his/her hair, how he/she walked, who his/her friends were, etc. Why did we do all these things? Because we really liked that person. For the believer, God is the most loved person or thing in our life; nothing or nobody is more important. Jesus said, *"He that loveth father or mother more than me is not worthy of me: and he that loveth son or daughter more than me is not worthy of me" (Matthew 10:37).* The study of God's word is how we come to know the heart of God, what He loves (and hates), how to be near Him, what puts a barrier between us, how to pray and why, God's character, and much more. It is through a careful study of the Bible that we begin to understand God, and we learn wisdom to live our lives in a way that pleases Him and blesses others. "But I already know God. Why do I have to study the Bible when I already know these things?" If you have never studied the Bible or had it taught to you thoroughly and carefully, then you don't know God. You only know what you have either been told or what you have come to believe without any basis to rely upon. God is only revealed through His word.

Paul wrote to his pupil, Timothy:

And that from a child thou hast known the holy scriptures, which are able to make thee wise unto salvation through faith which is in Christ Jesus. All scripture is given by inspiration of God, and is profitable for doctrine, for reproof, for correction, for instruction in righteousness: that the man of God may be perfect, thoroughly furnished unto all good works.

2 Timothy 3:15-17

Notice that the holy scriptures (the Bible) are able to make a person *"wise unto salvation."* The Bible leads the seeker, who studies the Bible for truth, to salvation. It will point that person to Jesus and the faith to believe. Notice also that in addition to salvation, the Bible is given by God's inspiration. The word "inspiration" has been translated from a Greek word that literally means "breathed." The scriptures are "God-breathed" so that they are the very words directly from God's mouth. Their purpose, after leading a soul to salvation, is found here; it provides the basis for sound doctrine, it corrects us when we err, it convicts us of our sin, and it instructs us. It does all of this so that we may grow in our faith and in our usefulness to God's kingdom. Notice the text says that as a result of exposure to the Bible, the man of God is "perfect," properly prepared and furnished to do good works. The word "perfect" does not mean that we reach a point that we never sin again. The word means "mature." In other words, as we continue studying the Bible, our faith grows stronger, we become wiser and more mature in our walk with God. This gives us the ability to serve God even better. No surprise that immediately after this passage, Paul told Timothy, *"I charge thee therefore before God, and the Lord Jesus Christ, who shall judge the quick and the dead at his appearing and his kingdom; preach the word"* (2 Timothy 4:1-2). Because God knows all of this, He has commanded us to study the Bible: *"Study to shew thyself approved unto God, a workman that needeth not to be ashamed, rightly dividing the word of truth"* (2 Timothy 2:15).

If you are new at trying to study the Bible, and if you have tried to read it but have struggled to understand what you are reading, then I recommend you find a good Bible commentary to lead you through your study. There are several good ones that do a wonderful job of taking the scriptures and explaining them. I recommend the Bible series by J. Vernon McGee entitled *Thru the Bible*; it is a five-volume set, and it goes through every book of the Bible, pretty much verse by verse. McGee was a gifted pastor who was rock solid in his teaching. If you find this set, it is well worth the investment. I would recommend that you read about two chapters per day, every single day. My suggestion would be to pray briefly about your study, then read your portion of the Bible slowly as you try to understand it. Then afterward, open up your Bible commentary and read the commentary while you "check" if your understanding was the same as the author. Over time, you will begin to see things you never saw or understood, and your faith will grow. I also recommend that you begin with the Gospel of *John* and work your way *slowly* through the New Testament before getting into *Genesis* and the Old Testament. Make up your mind and do it today and every day for the rest of your life! You'll never regret it.

CHAPTER 5

The Doctrine of the Trinity

Back in my undergraduate days at the University of Texas in Austin and while studying petroleum engineering, I was required to take upper-level math courses which featured increasingly complex equations and concepts. These became more and more difficult to understand the further I progressed in my studies, and my work to grasp these concepts became more and more difficult. At one point, I recall feeling that I could not reconcile the new ideas being introduced with what I thought I had already learned. That feeling left me in despair as to whether I would ever understand what the professor was trying to teach. (I never did learn some of those concepts.) In my experience in talking to many people about the doctrine of the triune nature of God, it seems the concept for most people is often equivalent to my upper-level college material. As a result, the doctrine of the Trinity is probably the most misunderstood doctrine in scripture. In this chapter and by God's grace, I shall endeavor to help simplify it and make it understandable.

The idea of the Trinity holds that God exists as three distinct "persons" who cooperatively and cohesively form one God. These three are the Father, the Son, and the Holy Ghost. *"For there are three that bear record in heaven, the Father, the Word, and the Holy Ghost: and these three are one" (1 John 5:7).* The doctrine holds that all three joined together comprise the God of the Bible. You might be surprised to discover that the word "trinity" does not appear in the Bible. From where then does this doctrine arise?

In my estimation, the best place to start when broaching this topic is in the writings of Moses. *"Hear, O Israel: The LORD our God is one LORD:" (Deuteronomy 6:4).* You may be asking: "What on earth does that verse have to do with our topic of the Trinity?" Everything. In this verse, God describes Himself: *The LORD our God is one LORD*; the description being the last two words of this sentence. The Hebrew word "echad" is what is translated as "one" in this text. Thus, the text reads: *The LORD our God is echad LORD.* "Echad" means to be united. It is the exact same word used by God to describe marriage when He states that the man and the woman shall be "one" flesh *(Genesis 2:24).* In the marriage passage, we have two individual persons united and becoming one. Thus, "echad" carries the meaning of unity among a plurality, such as nine baseball players making "one" team. Remember that all scripture is God-breathed (2 *Timothy* 3:16). Thus, God breathed the exact wording through Moses. God could have chosen the Hebrew word "Yachid," meaning a singular one, but He didn't. God's choice of the word "echad" was purposeful and accurate. So when God described Himself in the verse above, He was purposefully and specifically stating that God is a unity of persons.

In addition to writing *Deuteronomy*, Moses also wrote the four other books of the Bible, including the book of *Genesis*. Moses recorded a conversation during the creation of man when he wrote,

> And God said, Let us make man in our image, after our likeness: and let them have dominion over the fish of the sea, and over the fowl of the air, and over the cattle, and over all the earth, and over every creeping thing that creepeth upon the earth. So God created man in his own image, in the image of God created he him; male and female created he them.
>
> *Genesis 1:26-27*

There are two things to note in these verses regarding creation: 1) The creation of man was of God, but a plural God ("let *us* make man"), and 2) Man was created in the image of God, but once again a plural God ("after *our* likeness"). "Hold on," you may be saying. "God was talking to the angels here. That is why he used the word 'us.' Right?" No, not right. The angelic host has no part in the creation of anything. It was God alone who was the creator, and no other entity was involved in the creation.

> Thus saith the LORD, thy redeemer, and he that formed thee from the womb, I am the LORD that maketh all things; that stretcheth forth the heavens alone; that spreadeth abroad the earth by myself.
>
> *Isaiah 44:24*

Yet, in the *Genesis* passage above, God says creation was made by "us." Why? Because God exists as "echad" LORD, a perfect union among a plurality, which is the Father, the Son, and the Holy Ghost.

The Father

While it is generally accepted that the Father is God, I still think it beneficial to include a few passages that make this clear. In *John 3:16*, Jesus states, *"For God so loved the world, that he gave his only begotten Son, that whosoever believeth in him should not perish, but have everlasting life."*

43

Here we see a distinction made between God and "his only begotten Son." In the very next verse, Jesus continued: *"For God sent not his Son into the world to condemn the world; but that the world through him might be saved"* (John 3:17). Again, notice the distinction between the Father and the Son. But here, we also see something different: we see that God "sent" His Son. Jesus came to earth to give His life for the souls of men by following God the Father's instructions. In another passage, Jesus said, *"I can of mine own self do nothing: as I hear, I judge: and my judgment is just; because I seek not mine own will, but the will of the Father which hath sent me"* (John 5:30). In His earthly ministry, Jesus made it absolutely clear that He came to say and do what His Father instructed. (See also *John 4:34; John 8:25-29.*) There are many other passages that deal with the Father being God, and this concept is typically without dispute. The arguments and disputes normally arise when addressing the other two persons of the Godhead, Jesus and the Holy Spirit.

The Son

When the Christian faith was birthed after the crucifixion and resurrection of Jesus, the early church understood and believed that Jesus was God. They embraced the doctrine of the Trinity, causing the Jewish people to accuse the Christians of worshipping multiple gods. But as we shall see, this idea was not created by the early Christians but was outlined in the Old Testament scriptures long before Jesus' birth at Bethlehem. Still, the idea that God was comprised of more than one entity was very disturbing to the Jews (and to many other people!), and they resisted the concept.

I have heard people say over the years, "Jesus never claimed to be God, only the Son of God." Is that true? And does the Old Testament make any claims to the deity of Jesus? Let's start by looking at a dispute that arose during Jesus' earthly ministry. He had just healed a man on the Sabbath day (the day of God-ordered rest from work), who was thirty-eight years with a severe disability. The Jews then confronted Jesus about having this man carry his bed on this holy day of rest.

> But Jesus answered them, My Father worketh hitherto, and I work. Therefore the Jews sought the more to kill him, because he not only had broken the sabbath, but said also that God was his Father, making himself equal with God.
>
> *John 5:17-18*

The Jews at the time and in the heat of the argument understood that Jesus was claiming equality with God by claiming to be His Son. All people get their nature from their fathers, and as a result, we all have the same nature as our fathers. Jesus was no different, except that His Father was God.

While the Jewish leaders in Jesus' time rejected Jesus' claims of deity, a careful reading of many Old Testament passages reveals their truth. Jesus is everywhere in the Bible and is truly the central focus of the scriptures. (Jesus Himself said, *"Search the scriptures; for in them ye think ye have eternal life: and they are they which testify of me" (John 5:39)*. When He made this statement, there was no New Testament, only the writings of the Old Testament.) Let's look at few of those passages to see what they reveal:

> For unto us a child is born, unto us a son is given: and the government shall be upon his shoulder: and his name shall be called Wonderful, Counsellor, The mighty God, The everlasting Father, The Prince of Peace.
>
> *Isaiah 9:6*

Did you see it? The son who was to be born would be called The Mighty God. I have a relative who once told me, trying to explain that Jesus was not the God of the Bible, that Jesus was only The Mighty God and not the Almighty God. He said that Jehovah (the name of God) was not the Mighty God but the Almighty. This argument is silly as there are numerous places where Jeho-

vah is described as "mighty," such as *Deuteronomy 7:21,
10:17*, and *Genesis 49:24*, just to name a few. Seven hundred years before the birth of Jesus, Isaiah prophesied
that this Son who was to be born would be God. Isaiah
also spoke in *Isaiah 7:14*, stating that *"a virgin shall conceive, and bear a son, and shall call his name Immanuel"* We
are told by Matthew that Immanuel means "God with
us." (See *Matthew 1:23*.) Jesus was God walking among
humanity. Paul tells us in *Colossians* that all the fulness
of the Godhead was found in Jesus in His bodily form
(*Colossians 2:9*).

Now let's get back to our *Isaiah 9:6* passage cited
above. In that same Isaiah verse, the prophet also says
that one of the names of the Son to be born was "The everlasting Father." You rarely hear this name used for Jesus, yet the Bible claims that it properly belongs to Him.
The keyword here is "everlasting." It comes from the
Hebrew word "ad," which means "duration of perpetu-
ity" or "eternity." In other words, this Son to be born is
eternal in nature, which means He is not created. This
is the very essence of God since no other creature or
thing can make the same claim. John the Baptist would
later hint towards this truth when he stated, *"This was
he of whom I spake, He that cometh after me is preferred before me: for he was before me" (John 1:15)*. According to the
Bible, John the Baptist was six months older than Jesus.
Yet, John stated that "he was before me," a human im-

possibility if Jesus was just a man. But the Bible says Jesus was not just a man, He stepped into human history from eternity past.

In another familiar passage most often heard during the Christmas season, the prophet Micah stated,

> But thou, Bethlehem Ephratah, though thou
> be little among the thousands of Judah, yet
> out of thee shall he come forth unto me that is
> to be ruler in Israel; whose goings forth have
> been from of old, from everlasting.
>
> *Micah 5:2*

There is it again. The one who would be born in Bethlehem would be God's ruler in Israel, and His life did not commence when He was born in Bethlehem since He came out from "everlasting," that is, eternity past. No angel or man can make that statement, and this explains what John the Baptist was referring to in the passage above.

There are several other passages where the deity of Jesus is found, including some where Jesus takes the name of Jehovah. (See *Jeremiah 23:5-6; Isaiah 44:6; 45:11.*) "How can this be," you may be asking, "since Jehovah is the name for the Father?" That is true, but since they are one, they properly share the same name. "That doesn't sound right," you say? Are you married? I am. My wife's name was Mora before we got married. Her name since the ceremony is Ramirez, and so is mine. The day we got married and became one, we then had the same name. We are two distinct people today, but we have the same name, and by God's grace we remain one. The intimacy in the Godhead is much deeper than the best relationship any marriage could have, and there is no tension or disunion amongst the Father and the Son (and the Holy Ghost).

Now, as to Jesus never claiming He was God, let's take a look.

> I and my Father are one. Then the Jews took up stones again to stone him. Jesus answered them, Many good works have I showed you from my Father; for which of those do ye stone me? The Jews answered him, saying, For a good work we stone thee not; but for blasphemy; and because that thou, being a man, makest thyself God.
>
> *John 10:30-33*

The Jews who were present that day (and there were many of them) fully grasped that Jesus was claiming to be God during this confrontation, and they reminded Him of it when asked to justify their seeking to stone Him. Also, keep in mind that if God is Jesus' earthly

Father, Mary being overcome by the Holy Ghost and becoming pregnant, then Jesus has the nature of His Father. That nature had no sin, and no other man can make that claim either. There is *much* more that could be written using the scriptures to prove the deity of Jesus, but this is a writing on the fundamentals of the Christian faith, not an advanced study. As you spend more time studying the Bible daily, you will soon discover this truth is spread throughout the Bible.

The Holy Spirit

"Okay...so maybe Jesus is God, but where does the idea of the Holy Spirit being God come from?" First, in the beginning, the Holy Spirit was with God in the creation, as we see in *Genesis 1:2.* The Holy Spirit, therefore, was part of the work of creation. (For you advanced Bible students...I can hear you running to the book of Job to remind me that the angelic hosts were there when God created in *Genesis 1*, and they aren't God. That is true, but they had no part in the creation; they were only spectators. The Holy Spirit played an active role.) As we saw earlier in this chapter, God was the sole creator. Thus, if the Holy Spirit played an active part, He must be God.

Another passage that reveals this truth is found in the book of *Acts.* In this book, it is recorded what occurred when a married couple came to Peter to offer only a portion of a sum they had pledged to God and lied about it:

> But Peter said, Ananias, why hath Satan filled thine heart to lie to the Holy Ghost, and to keep back part of the price of the land? Whiles it remained, was it not thine own? and after it was sold, was it not in thine own power? why hast thou conceived this thing in thine heart? thou hast not lied unto men, but unto God.
>
> *Acts 5:3-4*

The husband lied to the Holy Ghost and not to men... he lied to God.

Furthermore, when Paul writes about spiritual gifts, he said that there are different spiritual gifts (to be used for God's kingdom) but only one Spirit. (*1 Corinthians 12:4.*) Paul goes on to itemize some of the gifts that are given to men, such as wisdom, knowledge, healing, etc. Then he states: *"But all these worketh that one and the selfsame Spirit, dividing to every man severally as he will"* (1 Corinthians 12:11). Notice here that it is the same Holy Spirit that provides men with these different gifts and skills, and He provides them to every man "as he will." This means that according to Paul, it is the Holy Spirit who decides who will be provided with what gifts and skillsets as He chooses. In other words, the Holy Spirit has complete authority in making these decisions. Paul then goes on to explain how all believers cannot have the same gifts, or the body of Jesus would not function as it should. If everybody was an eye, then the body could not feel, or hear, or walk. Different people have to be provided with different skills and gifts. Later in the same chapter, Paul goes on to say, *"But now hath God set the members every one of them in the body, as it hath pleased him" (1 Corinthians 12:18)*. Notice in this verse that it is God who provides the believers with their skillsets. Well, we either have a complete contradiction in the Bible, or the Holy Spirit is God. (Hint: there are no contradictions in the Bible, and anyone who says otherwise doesn't know what they are talking about.) There are other passages that support the Holy Spirit being God, but again, this is not an advanced study.

The Father, the Son, and the Holy Ghost are all God individually, yet they form the one (echad) God of the Bible as a unit. There is no contradiction nor disagreement in the Godhead, only total agreement, love, fellowship, harmony, and unity. Still, there is an order to their unity. Jesus willingly submits to the authority and headship of God the Father, even though He is an equal. When speaking of the ultimate end of the world, Paul writes, *"And when all things shall be subdued unto him [Jesus], then shall the Son also himself be subject to him [God the Father] that put all things under him, that God may be all in all"* (1 Corinthians 15:28) *(brackets added for clarity).* In the end, Jesus will submit to the rule of the Father. Total humility and total submission from one equal to another. It is amazing! Rarely, if ever, is this seen in the human realm. Christians do not worship three gods; Bible-believing Christians worship the Father, the Son, and the Holy Ghost, who together are "one *LORD.*"

CHAPTER 6

Prayer: What is It and is It Necessary?

True friends are rare, for a true friend will stay by your side through whatever highs and lows life may bring. They don't scatter when trouble arises, they feel your pain when you weep and your joy when you celebrate, and they genuinely love you. For those of us who have had the honor of having such friends, we have surely spent countless hours talking with these true friends about everything imaginable, freely and without reservation. We don't guard our words or our emotions when we are with them, sharing all that is deep in our hearts and on our minds while time washes swiftly away. These friends listen carefully to all we share and provide whatever guidance or wisdom they can. All done in love for us. Prayer is exactly the same thing, with God being our rarest of true friends.

The Bible says that *"there is a friend that sticketh closer than a brother" (Proverbs 18:24).* This is a reference to Jesus, who would later say:

> Henceforth I call you not servants; for the servant knoweth not what his lord doeth: but I have called you friends; for all things that I have heard of my Father I have made known unto you.
>
> *John 15:15*

A friendship is an intimate relationship that runs deep. It binds two souls in a unique way that no other can appreciate or gauge, and in the midst of their time together, nothing is off-limits. Each knows the other will protect and guard all that is shared, and none other shall intrude into the sanctity of that union. What a privilege it is to be called "friends" by Almighty God!

When Jesus was dying on the cross, He was paying the full price for the redemption of our souls. At the moment He died, the Bible states, *"And, behold, the veil of the temple was rent in twain from the top to the bottom; and the earth did quake, and the rocks rent" (Matthew 27:51).* Why is this strange fact about the tearing of the veil inserted into the gospel record? Before that question is answered and to fully appreciate its significance, we need to look back into a bit of Jewish history.

When God had taken the Israelites out of Egypt and led them through the desert on their way to the promised land, God instructed Moses to fabricate and erect a tabernacle which would be in the midst of the Jewish camp and would be the focal point of their worship of God. The instructions that God gave to Moses were very specific, giving details down to fabric, colors, location, materials, and dimensions, among numerous other things. In this construction blueprint outlined by God, Moses was to construct the entire complex, which would consist of a single door leading into an Outer Court, which in turn led to an Inner Court (see Diagram "A").

Within the Outer Court were two articles of furniture overlaid with brass. It is here that the sin of man was to be dealt with at the first article of furniture that would be encountered, the Brass Alter. The priests would perform their functions as God had laid them out. Afterward, the priests would then move to the second article of furniture, the Brass Laver, to wash and ceremonially be clean before God as they continued in the performance of their duties. It is only after the priest would be cleansed that he could enter into the Inner Court.

Within the Inner Court, brass would no longer be found; here, everything was made of gold. Three articles

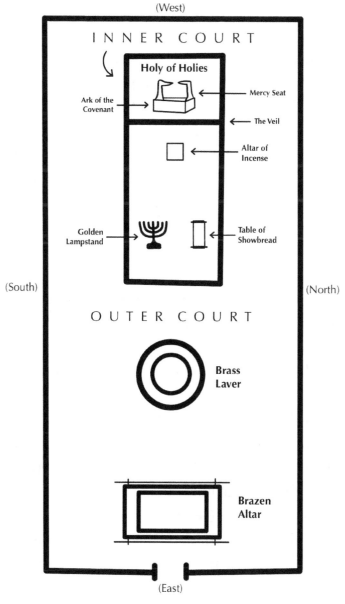

Diagram A

of furniture would be encountered when entering the Golden Lampstand, the Altar of Incense, and the Table of Shewbread. Here the priests would minister before God, each article of furniture representing a different facet of the person and work of Jesus Christ. Priests moved through this area daily. Yet within the Inner Court lay a more secluded chamber where nobody was allowed to enter, except for the High Priest himself and only on one day per year! This chamber was known as The Holy of Holies, and in it resided two final articles of furniture: the Ark of the Covenant and the Mercy Seat. It is here that God resided. (See *Exodus 25:22; 1 Chronicles 13:6.*) But, God had commanded that a veil be placed between the Holy of Holies and the main room of the Inner Court where the other three articles of furniture were located. (See *Exodus 26:33.*) The veil was constructed of different materials in the exact specifications outlined by God, and its purpose was to separate sinful man from holy God. In other words, the veil made certain that no man would be allowed into God's presence except for the High Priest and only once a year (and he had to bring blood). (See *Hebrews 9:7.*) This was the reality of life in the Jewish world that was well understood: God was separated from sinful man, and the two could not be joined.

Now back to the question raised earlier: why the strange fact about the veil being torn in two pieces, from the top to the bottom, at the moment Jesus died? The reason is that Jesus' death tore away the barrier that had separated God from man. Mankind now had free and open access to God. What a concept! God was no longer inaccessible to the human race. Jesus' sacrificial death made it possible to approach God. This is exactly what defines prayer. *"Let us therefore come boldly unto the throne of grace, that we may obtain mercy, and find grace to help in time of need" (Hebrews 4:16).* We now have standing to appear before God in the name and the power of Jesus to make our requests to God.

"But," you may be asking, "didn't people come to God through prayer before Jesus' death?" Of course, they did. "Well, then how could prayer be opened up only through Jesus' death if it was already happening before?" I did not say that Jesus' death opened up the pathway of prayer; prayer was already in place before Jesus' death, but it had to be brought from afar. You see, in the Inner Court was the Altar of Incense, which pictures, among other things, prayer. But the prayer was brought from outside of the veil, again, separated from God by the veil. Now, after Jesus' death, no longer was there a need to bring the prayer from afar; people who believed could now come directly to God's throne to make their petitions.

The Purpose of Prayer

Now Jesus made clear that God already knows what we need before we ask Him. (See *Matthew 6:8.*) So, then, what is the point of prayer? Prayer serves three major purposes: it demonstrates a believer's reliance on God's grace, mercy, and provision; it provides for intimate communion with God, and it practices obedience to God's lordship.

By bringing prayers to God, we acknowledge that it is God who provides us with His grace, mercy, and provision. He forgives our sins when we confess them in prayer to God, thus extending us mercy. (See *1 John 1:9.*) He supplies us with wisdom and direction when we ask Him in prayer, thus extending to us one aspect of His grace (and there are many others). (See *James 1:5.*) He provides for all our needs, thus supplying us with all our provisions. (See *Matthew 6:31-33.*) If we pray only in this area, not only for ourselves but also for others in our hearts, our prayer time will grow quickly. But prayer doesn't end here.

By now, we have learned that according to the Bible, Jesus was God while He walked this earth. He was fully God and, at the same time, fully man. Yet, the Bible makes clear that Jesus took time to pray. He would rise early and pray before He got His day going, and He would pray late. (See *Luke 6:12; Matthew 14:23.*) But why? If Jesus was God, then what would be the point of His prayers? The answer is communion. Jesus was having intimate time with God the Father, without any distractions. If you look at the verses referenced in Luke and Matthew, you will notice that He prayed alone in the mountains. Nobody or nothing to distract Him from His prayer time with God. This is the same type of intimacy that one has with a true friend, only Jesus' intimacy with God the Father is much closer! This would be where Jesus was most at peace and where He would be strengthened and encouraged. This is another reason we pray. We, too, need our "alone time" with God. We need that intimacy where our love for God can grow, as can our faith. It is a time where we can give thanks to God for all His mercy and provision and a time when we can praise God for who He is and the things He has done (and will do). The Christian life and the natural life are polar opposites: in the natural life, we are born helpless and must rely totally on our parents to provide all we need. As we grow older, we get stronger and gain more and more independence, eventually reaching the point where we no longer need anyone to provide for us. In the Christian life, it is exactly opposite. We are "born again," and yet we are very independent, not really understanding our need for God and His provision. As we grow, we learn more about God and His Word, and we become more and more dependent on God to provide for our needs and our direction. Eventually, we reach a point of such intimacy that we simply curl up in the bosom of God, and by faith, we totally rely on God providing everything we need. That is intimacy, and it breeds deep faith! This is an important part of spending time in prayer.

We also pray because we are commanded to do so. *"Pray without ceasing" (1 Thessalonians 5:17; see also Ephesians 6:18).* We pray for all the reasons referenced above, but we also do so because God requires it. It is through prayer that God's power is unleashed, even today. *"For the weapons of our warfare are not carnal, but mighty through God to the pulling down of strong holds" (2 Corinthians 10:4).* Notice that the weapons of the Christian are not "carnal"; that is, they are not earthly weapons that can be wielded by the flesh. The weapon for the Christian is prayer, and it is spiritual; it is mighty and much damage can be inflicted upon the enemies of God through it. But the prayer must be lifted to make an impact. The Bible also states, *"The effectual fervent prayer of a righteous man availeth much" (James 5:16).* Here, we are told that fervent and persistent prayer does much good. It has been said that the power of God is unleashed through prayer. There are thousands upon thousands of stories of people who prayed, and the power of God was unleashed, totally removing cancer cells, baffling doctors, healing people who were told they would surely die, and saving the souls of some of the most rebellious persons to live. All of these miracles were because somebody, or a group of somebodies, prayed.

Real prayer is strenuous work for the body, as the mind must be disciplined to regularly engage in fervent prayer while the body has no such desire. Like every other discipline that requires vigorous work, it is a constant struggle to remain faithful in prayer day after day and year after year. For the spirit, however, there is no such struggle. The spirit basks in the glory and the presence of God while an individual is engaged in true prayer, freely resting in the everlasting arms of God. It is at ease, and as a result, many have found themselves in prayer for hours in a single prayer session.

Lastly, how should we pray? Jesus was asked the same question in *Luke 11:1*. He responded by stating,

> When ye pray, say, Our Father which art in heaven, Hallowed be thy name. Thy kingdom come. Thy will be done, as in heaven, so in earth. Give us day by day our daily bread. And forgive us our sins; for we also forgive every one that is indebted to us. And lead us not into temptation; but deliver us from evil.
>
> *Luke 11:2-4*

Here we find a familiar passage that many of us have learned from our youth. Indeed, many recite this prayer so often that they never really stop to ponder its meaning. But Jesus was not providing us a prayer to recite; instead, He was providing us with a model of how to pray. Consequently, this prayer is rightly called the model prayer. Notice the first part of the prayer, *"Our Father which art in heaven, Hallowed by thy name."* This section represents humility before God as well as prayer and praise. We are humbled because God is the lofty One; He resides in heaven (we don't), and His name is to be hallowed, which means it is to be venerated or sanctified as pure and holy. This is praise. So a portion of our prayers should be dedicated to our humility before God and praise to God.

The next section asks for God to bring His kingdom to the earth. *"Thy kingdom come. Thy will be done, as in heaven, so in earth."* Today, kingdoms of men are in power. The day is coming, however, when God's kingdom will be brought to this very earth, and Jesus Himself will rule it with a rod of iron for a thousand years. (See *Daniel 2:44; Psalm 2*.) As part of our prayers, we seek God to establish His kingdom on the earth. We also ask for God to have His will done all over this earth. Today, lawlessness and violence cover the earth. We are wanting God to change all of that so that His will (love, peace, joy, thanksgiving, and the other fruits of the spirit as found in *Galatians 5:22-23*) is the normal behavior on this planet.

Jesus then moves the prayer into the next section, *"Give us day by day our daily bread."* Here we come before God, acknowledging that He is our provider; He is the one who makes sure we have all that we need to live, and so we bring these prayers before Him, asking for His provision in all we require. Many people fail to recognize that it is God who provides us everything we have. Many have made the tragic mistake of believing that their futures are secure because of the financial plan they have developed over the years, and they fail to realize that the money accumulated and saved up over the years can disappear overnight. This is easily seen in the early 1920s when the German people lost everything due to hyperinflation; a lifetime of savings was gone in an instant. The same is true for the people of Mexico during the late 1980s when the value of the peso deflated. Money is not security; money is a tool. True believers understand that the only true security we have is God. He will provide, and we come to Him in prayer seeking that provision.

The next section of the prayer deals with our sin. *"And forgive us our sins; for we also forgive every one that is indebted to us."* We are to take time in our prayers to confess our sins so that God will forgive us. The Bible says, *"If we confess our sins, he is faithful and just to forgive us our sins, and to cleanse us from all unrighteousness"* (1 John 1:9). If we don't take time to confess our sins, then our prayers are ineffective because of the barrier that separates us from God; that barrier is our sin. *"If I regard iniquity in my heart, the Lord will not hear me"* (Psalm 66:18). In other words, if I am carrying sin in my life and it is not confessed, God will not hear my prayers. I must have that sin barrier removed so that God will be receptive and attentive to my prayers. But notice Jesus' words in the model prayer stating that we also forgive everyone that is indebted to us. This means that we also forgive every person that has sinned against us. This is very important because if there is somebody in your life that you have not forgiven or will not forgive, God will not forgive you either. This truth is crystal clear in the Bible as taught by Jesus when He said, *"For if ye forgive men their trespasses, your heavenly Father will also forgive you: but if ye forgive not men their trespasses, neither will your Father forgive your trespasses"* (Matthew 6:14-15). (See also *Matthew 18:21-35.*) James put it this way: *"For he shall have judgment without mercy, that hath shewed no mercy"* (James 2:13). So before you ask God for the forgiveness of your sins in prayer, make sure that you have first forgiven all who have sinned against you!

In the last section, Jesus said, *"And lead us not into temptation; but deliver us from evil."* Here, we pray that God keeps us away from trials that often bring hurt, struggle, and fear to our lives. Understand, however, that sometimes God wants us to go through the trial, for it is through trials that we learn patience and reliance on God's grace. (*James 1:2-3.*) But God will not permit that we endure a trial that is beyond our ability to handle, as He confirms in *1 Corinthians 10:13*. Nevertheless, we pray that we don't have to enter into such trials. We also pray for God's protection so that He keeps us away from the devil and his henchmen. No demon is able to attack a child of God without permission from God. This is seen clearly in *Job 1* and 2. So we take time to pray for His protection from the dark forces that are constantly on the move looking to devour souls. *"Be sober, be vigilant; because your adversary the devil, as a roaring lion, walketh about, seeking whom he may devour"* (1 Peter 5:8).

The topics Jesus outlined in the model prayer are different areas to be addressed in our prayers, but there are plenty of others too. This list is not exclusive. Other topics can include people who are sick, ministry work, missionaries, neighbors, co-workers, salvation for the lost, and many other such things. Now you can see how true prayer can be burdensome and time-consuming. "So if we aren't supposed to recite the prayer Jesus taught daily, how do you propose it should be done?" I hear you asking. Well, what type of conversations do you have with your best friends? Most of us do not have conversations with our friends where we simply repeat the same things over and over again. It wouldn't be much of a conversation, would it? If prayer is intimacy with God, then we need to lift prayers that are direct and honest. They should not be lifted with flowery and picturesque language. Jesus said,

> But when ye pray, use not vain repetitions, as the heathen do: for they think that they shall be heard for their much speaking. Be not ye therefore like unto them: for your Father knoweth what things ye have need of, before ye ask him.
>
> *Matthew 6:7-8*

Open your heart to God when you pray. Tell Him all that is troubling you; tell Him all about your sins that you've committed and repent before Him; tell Him how marvelous and gracious and merciful He is, as you lift up praises to God; tell Him how you need His wisdom to handle all things that cross your path; tell Him that certain people you know need His grace and mercy; and on and on the list goes. This is how we proceed in our prayer life, all the while looking and listening for God's response. This is an integral part of the Christian life, and anyone who chooses not to take it seriously does so at their own peril.

CHAPTER 7

Was It Really Necessary for Jesus to Die?

There are certain things we have all encountered in our lives that just don't seem to make sense, such as how gravity works, why the designated hitter was introduced into baseball, and the existence of Daylight Savings Time (just to name a few). If you have ever been around a church for very long, then you have surely heard the saying that Jesus died for our sins. But how does that make any sense at all? Even more frustrating is that when pressed as to why Jesus had to die, most Christians cannot give a good reason or explanation. Was it really necessary for Jesus to suffer and die for our sins? If you ask these questions to different people, you will typically get varied responses. There are several things among professing Christians which most do not fully appreciate or comprehend, in my estimation, two of which are: (1) the suffering, both physically and spiritually, of Jesus Christ during His passion, and (2) the reason all this suffering was necessary. In this chapter, we will explore what the Bible reveals as to why it was really necessary for Jesus Christ to die. In the next chapter, we will study his suffering.

Sin Enters the World

The story is told in *Genesis 3* how Adam and Eve sinned against God by eating from the tree of knowledge of good and evil, which God had specifically forbidden them to do. Prior to this disobedient act, Adam and Eve lived in a paradise where there was no death, sickness, disease, hatred, or other offspring of sin. Adam and Eve were pure and clean; there was no sin in them or the Garden. Everything was perfect. However, God had warned Adam, *"But of the tree of knowledge of good and evil, thou shalt not eat of it: for in the day that thou eatest thereof thou shalt surely die" (Genesis 2:17).* It is evident that Eve was also given this warning since she responded with such knowledge to the serpent as he weaved his deceptive web to ensnare her. (See *Genesis 3:3.*) But as the Bible records, Adam and Eve did eat from the forbidden tree, and sin entered the Garden paradise. At the exact time that the fruit was eaten, Adam and Eve died just as God had warned. "Wait a minute!" you may be saying. "They clearly did *not* die because the Bible says that

they continued to live and had children." You are correct. They did not immediately die physically, although
their bodies began the process of dying. However, they
immediately became *spiritually* dead since they became
separated from God.[1] Remember what Paul said while
addressing believers,

> And you hath he quickened [made alive], who
> were dead in trespasses and sins; wherein in
> time past ye walked according to the course
> of this world, according to the prince of the
> power of the air, the spirit that now worketh
> in the children of disobedience.
>
> *Ephesians 2:1-2* (brackets added for clarity)

Did you catch that? Paul was saying that all people
are *dead* in trespasses and sins until they are given new
life by believing in the finished work of Jesus on the
cross, meaning that we are all separated from God until we become true believers. In other words, we are all

1 A study of the Bible will reveal that all death is defined as the
separation of two things. In the first death (which everybody goes
through), the soul inside a person is separated from the body
against its will. (See James 2:26.) In the second death (which only
the unbelievers will go through), the same soul is eternally separated against its will from the presence of God. (See Revelation
20:11-15.) Thus, at the time a person dies, the soul inside immediately separates from the body, and the body becomes lifeless. It is
very much like an electric toy run by batteries; once the batteries
are removed, the toy is "dead" for all purposes until good batteries
are put back inside it. The same is true for every human being; once
the soul is removed, the body no longer has any life in it.

dead until we become saved. This is exactly what God meant when he said Adam and Eve would die that very day if they ate from the forbidden tree.

The penalty for sin as decreed by God is stated very clearly in *Romans 6:23, "The wages of sin is death,"* and in *Ezekiel 18:20, "The soul that sinneth, it shall die."*

Thus, the penalty for sin was immediately imposed upon Adam and Eve. No longer would Adam be able to take leisurely walks with God in the cool of the day as he had done before, and his body began the process of decaying and physically dying. The consequences of this rebellion were severe and would impact the entire human race that was yet to be born; every single person born after this initial sin would be a sinner by birth. *"Wherefore, as by one man sin entered into the world, and death by sin; and so death passed upon all men, for that all have sinned" (Romans 5:12).* Here we see that through Adam, sin entered into the world as did death, and that same death was passed through Adam's genetic line to all who were later born. Everybody ever born after Adam and Eve was automatically born into sin. (For a more detailed explanation, see Chapter 2, *Was Man Born With Original Sin?*) Every person who has ever lived (without exception) has been guilty of sin before God, and the Bible makes this perfectly clear. *"As it is written, There is none righteous, no, not one:" (Romans 3:10); "For all have sinned, and come short of the glory of God" (Romans*

3:23); "But the scripture hath concluded all under sin" (Ga-latians 3:22); "All we like sheep have gone astray; we have turned every one to his own way" (Isaiah 53:6). All mankind, therefore, was headed for the penalty of death, the eternal separation from God in a terrifying place the Bible calls "hell."

The Sacrifice for Sin

God had mapped out a plan to save the world from sin even before He had created the world (see *Revelation 13:8; 2 Timothy 1:9; Ephesians 1:4-5*), and that plan required the shedding of blood. After all, the penalty for sin, which was decreed by God, had to be carried out... the sinner had to die. *"And almost all things are by the law purged with blood; and without shedding of blood is no remission"* (Hebrews 9:22). But why was bloodshed necessary to forgive mankind's sins? Couldn't God find another way to forgive mankind without bloodshed? After all, God is supreme, right? Why couldn't He just make a declaration that He was forgiving mankind's sin and was giving the human race a second chance? Was it really necessary for Jesus to leave the glory of heaven, lay aside His royal robes of deity, be born a man, and purposefully go to the cross to be slaughtered? The answer from God's holy word is clearly yes.

Before we explore the scriptures to discover why Jesus needed to die, let me ask two questions. (1) Can God do anything? (2) Is there any limit to his actions? These may seem like trick questions, but they are not. The correct answers are no and yes, respectively. "What can't God do?" you may be asking. Simple, God cannot sin! He cannot do anything which is contrary to His sinless, holy nature. For example, in *Titus 1:2*, Paul states that God cannot lie. God cannot accept sin or even look upon sin. *"Art thou not from everlasting, O LORD, my God, mine Holy One? Thou art of purer eyes than to behold evil, and canst not look on iniquity [sin]:" (Habakkuk 1:12; 13) (brackets added).* His nature would not be holy if He could simply disregard His own word and give mankind a second chance without somebody paying the penalty for the sin. By doing such a thing, He would be violating His own laws and decrees, something He cannot do. *Psalm 22*, which we will examine more closely below, makes this clear. This Psalm presents a very graphic picture of the crucifixion from Christ's perspective as He is hanging on the cross. The first three verses are as follows:

> My God, my God, why hast thou forsaken me? Why art thou so far from helping me, and from the words of my roaring? O my God, I cry in the daytime, but thou hearest not; and in the night season, and am not silent. But thou art holy, O thou that inhabitest the praises of Israel.
>
> *Psalm 22:1-3 (emphasis added)*

You may recognize the first verse of this psalm: it was shouted by Jesus as He hung on the cross, as recorded in the Gospels *Matthew* and *Mark*. Remember, this psalm is written from Jesus' perspective as He hung on the cross. Why did God "forsake" Him as He hung on the cross? To "forsake" means to turn away from. Why was God so far from helping Him and from hearing His cries of agony? Because at the time Jesus was hanging on the cross, <u>He had become sin</u>, and God could not look upon Him due to God's holy nature, as we saw earlier through the Old Testament prophet Habakkuk. *"For he hath made him to be sin for us, who knew no sin; that we might be made the righteousness of God in him"* (2 Corinthians 5:21). *"Christ hath redeemed us from the curse of the law, being made a curse for us: for it is written, Cursed is every one that hangeth on a tree"* (Galatians 3:13). At the time that Christ hung on that cross, He had become a curse before God. "That's crazy!" you may be thinking. "Jesus became a curse!" He surely did. He became that curse by taking our sins onto Himself. As stated above, He who knew no sin became sin for us. As Jesus began His passion and which ended with Him nailed to the cross, a supernatural transaction was happening which no eye could see, save the eye of God Himself. The sins of all mankind who ever lived and ever would live were being drawn into the person of Jesus. The sin of man is ugly, and a stench in the nostrils of God, and Jesus absorbed it all. *Isaiah 53:6* says, *"The LORD hath laid on him the iniquity [sin] of us all" (brackets added)*. In essence, God turned His back on Christ at the hour He hung on that rugged cross because God cannot look upon or accept the presence of sin. This may sound difficult to believe, but it is true. Our God is a *Holy* God, as it states in *Psalm 22* above!

It has been established that a holy God cannot accept sin and therefore requires that a penalty of death be paid for the sin in blood. But why did Jesus, God in the flesh, have to be the sacrifice? Why couldn't someone else do it; someone, who actually deserved it? Well, if God had the actual sinner suffer the penalty, then there could never be reconciliation between that sinner and God. God needed a sacrifice that would satisfy the penalty that had to be imposed and still bring the human race to Him. In keeping with His holy nature, God required that the sacrificial lamb be *without spot and without blemish*. (See *Exodus 12:5; Leviticus 23:12*.) What person walking on this earth was without spot or blemish (in other words, sinless)? Nobody! Again, all have sinned and come short of the glory of God; there is none righteous, no not one (remember the passages above). As such, God was left with two choices that were in keeping with His holy nature. First, He could give each of us what we deserve...justice based on our individual works. However, only the people who were not born in sin and who were absolutely perfect (sinless) throughout their lives could be saved. Anybody who sinned even once could not be saved in keeping with God's holy nature. This is confirmed in *James 2:10*, where it states, *"For whosoever shall keep the whole law, and yet offend in one point, he is guilty of all."* This choice, therefore, would have resulted in the eternal doom of all mankind because nobody was ever born without sin and lived without actually sinning.

The second choice available to God was that He could have a sinless human be the sacrifice to pay for all the sins of mankind; a proxy or scapegoat who could carry the sin load for everybody else and who could suffer the punishment of death that the word of God demanded. The problem, as we have just seen, is that nobody in the human race has ever qualified to be that sinless, spotless sacrifice. Therefore, God had to take drastic and tough action to solve this problem. He was forced to send Jesus Christ from heaven to become a man and offer Himself, perfect, pure, and without blemish, as a blood sacrifice for all mankind; thus satisfying the penalty for our sins that God's holiness required and giving us the opportunity to live eternally with Him. Because of His deep love for us, He chose the second option, and I praise Him and thank Him for it daily. Have you ever really thought about that famous verse of scripture, *John 3:16: "For God so loved the world, that he gave his only begotten Son, that whosoever believeth in him should not perish, but have everlasting life.*"? Here the Bible makes it clear that God chose the second option...He loves us so much that He sent Christ to die on our behalf instead of letting us die eternally. That is the reason that Jesus had to die for us...*because nobody else could do it and still satisfy the requirements of God's holiness.*

> Yet it pleased the LORD to bruise him; he hath put him [Jesus] to grief: when thou shalt make his [Jesus'] soul an offering for sin, he shall see his seed, he shall prolong his days, and the pleasure of the LORD shall prosper in his hand. He [God the Father] shall see of the travail of his soul, and shall be satisfied: by his knowledge shall my righteous servant justify many; for he shall bear their iniquities.
> *Isaiah 53:10-11* (brackets and emphasis added)

Hallelujah! What a Savior!

CHAPTER 8

The Suffering of Jesus

We just saw in the last chapter that it was absolutely necessary for Jesus to die in order to redeem the souls of men and that by doing so, He became the scapegoat and took all our sins upon Himself. But in order to be the scapegoat for us and pay the penalty for all that sin, Jesus Christ ultimately suffered far more than any man in history. This conclusion is inevitable after a careful examination of the scriptures. He suffered both physically and spiritually, and the depths of His suffering simply cannot be fully comprehended by man. This short chapter attempts to provide better insight into the price Jesus paid for our salvation and why God has stated that the penalty will be severe for any individual who rejects Jesus. (See *Hebrews 10:29*.)

At the time of the Passover supper, which Jesus shared with his apostles in the upper room, Jesus was fully aware of the intense trials that would soon be a reality. *"Hereafter I will not talk much with you: for the prince of this world cometh, and hath nothing in me"* (John 14:30). Afterward, He took Peter, James, and John with Him to the Garden of Gethsemane to pray. The scriptures say, *"And he taketh with him Peter and James and John, began to be sore amazed, and to be very heavy; and saith unto them, My soul is exceeding sorrowful unto death: tarry ye here, and watch"* (Mark 14:33-34). The Bible says He fell to the ground and prayed. Notice His prayer. *"Father, if thou be willing, remove this cup from me: nevertheless not my will, but thine, be done"* (Luke 22:42). The agony and spiritual suffering He was to endure had Him very sorrowful to the point that He asked if the Father was willing to remove the task from Him which lay ahead. By the way, what would have happened if the cup had been removed by the Father? Then we would still be in our sins and would have no chance to be saved; we would all have to perish in our own sins! That is why Jesus continued His prayer by stating, "nevertheless not my will, but thine, be done." Luke continues,

> And there appeared an angel unto him from heaven, strengthening him. And being in an agony he prayed more earnestly: and his sweat was as it were great drops of blood falling down to the ground.
>
> *Luke 22:43-44*

Medical science tells us that on certain rare occasions when a person is extremely distressed, the membranes that separate the bloodstream from the sweat pores sometimes rupture and cause a person to sweat drops of blood. This is, apparently, what happened to Jesus that night in the Garden of Gethsemane.

Why was Jesus in such agony? He hadn't begun to suffer physically yet, so what was causing His pain? I believe there are two reasons for His suffering in the Garden. First, Jesus Christ, who was God in the flesh, was totally and completely holy. He had an absolutely pure nature, and He had never known sin or experienced sin. In fact, He could not sin because He was God. The main reason for His agony, I believe, is that Jesus knew that He was going to bear all of the sins of the world, past, present, and future, on Himself. As Paul stated, *"For he hath made him to be sin for us, who knew no sin; that we might be made the righteousness of God in him"* (2 Corinthians 5:21). Jesus knew that He was going to become sin and that He would be separated from God the Father, as we read in *Psalm 22:1-2*. For the first and only time in eternity, the Father, the Son, and the Holy Ghost would not be in harmonious unity; the Godhead would soon be fractured. Knowing this was the greatest agony that Jesus underwent spiritually.

The second reason is that Jesus, while still one hundred percent God, was also one hundred percent human. He went through the same things we go through, yet He was without sin. (See *Hebrews 4:15*.) Jesus knew exactly the type of death He was going to have to endure for the salvation of mankind, and this had to trouble Him. Just imagine the type of worry and stress you would endure if you knew that you were going to have to suffer a punishment that required the smashing of both your hands, one at a time, with a hammer or a door or a vice or something very painful. You would be very worried, especially as the time drew closer for the imposition of the punishment. Jesus' death would be infinitely more painful than that! Jesus knew exactly what was going to happen to Him; He indicated as much numerous times to His apostles, and this must have weighed heavily on his mind, knowing that it was about to begin. Jesus had said,

> I lay down my life for the sheep. No man taketh it from me, but I lay it down of myself. I have power to lay it down, and I have power to take it again. This commandment have I received of my Father.
>
> *John 10:15, 18*

Nobody took Jesus' life; He willingly laid it down in obedience to the Father's will in order that we might be saved.

Before Jesus ever got to Pilate, he had already been worn down. The scriptures show that Jesus had not slept in over twenty-four hours, and he had been brutally beaten by the servants of the Sanhedrin as part of a game they played. (See *Mark 14:65.*) Remember, Jesus never fought back, and He never hid his face or body from any blows. (See *Isaiah 50:6.*) By the time Jesus got to Pilate, He was already battered, beaten, and exhausted.

Now there are some very interesting and worthwhile truths that come from the study of Pilate while he was dealing with Jesus, but that is another study altogether. The Bible records that Pilate gave in to the pressure to crucify Jesus even though he clearly stated several times that he could find no fault in Jesus. Prior to His being crucified, however, Pilate ordered that He be scourged. It was surely a miracle when Jesus Christ died on the cross for my sins, but it was equally a miracle that Jesus even made it to the cross at Calvary without dying first. Now in order to fully appreciate this statement, you must understand the Roman concept of scourging. When somebody was scourged, they were whipped. But the Romans did not simply use a regular whip that you and I may be familiar with. Their whips had about nine to ten leather straps at the end, which would slam into the target, each strap woven through with pieces of jagged bone chips and/or small metal balls. You can imagine the damage that each full swing of that "whip" would make on its target as the bone chips dug into the flesh of the victim. Also, before the scourging began, the prisoner would be stretched out completely by tying his feet to the ground and his hands to a rope that ran overhead and was pulled on to stretch the person as much as possible. Jesus endured so many lashes that every one of his bones would be ultimately exposed, as stated in *Psalm 22:17*, "*I may tell all my bones: they look and stare upon me.*" For a person to "tell" all his bones simply means that he could count them all. My friend, Jesus must have lost massive amounts of blood during the scourging phase alone. It is no wonder that Jesus was unable to carry his crossbeam to Golgotha, where he was crucified, and that a bystander had to be pressed into service by the Roman soldiers to carry it for Him. (See *Mark 15:21*.)

After the scourging, you would think that the guards would have had mercy on this innocent man who is missing chunks of flesh and is bleeding profusely. But notice that after the scourging,

> And the soldiers led him away into the hall, called Praetorium; and they call together the whole band. And they clothed him with purple [a purple robe], and platted a crown of thorns, and put it about his head, and began

to salute him, Hail, King of the Jews! And they
smote him [hit him] on the head with a reed,
and did spit upon him, and bowing their
knees worshipped him.

Mark 15:16-19 (brackets added for clarity)

They continued to abuse Him in brutal fashion, and
after their twisted mocking, they led Him away to be
crucified.

The Romans considered death by crucifixion to
be the most painful death that one could endure, and
Psalm 22 makes this clear. Let us look more closely at
the crucifixion as employed by the Romans.[2] First of
all, not all prisoners were the same size, so each cross
was individually measured according to each person's
height. With the cross bar upon His shoulders, the soldiers would have dropped Jesus on His back in order to
measure where the crossbar needed to be placed on top
of the long, standing beam. The goal of the soldiers was
to have the person stretched as much as possible when
nailed to the cross, for reasons we shall see shortly. Once
this measurement was made, then Jesus was stood back
up, and His feet were nailed with an iron shank to the
long standing beam of the cross which would have been
lying on the ground. With His feet firmly nailed on the

---

2 This information is taken from the studies of Dr. David Wood, of
David Wood Ministries.

long beam of the cross, He was then dropped back to the ground on His back where His hands were nailed to the crossbar, which had been previously attached at the proper spot to the long beam. The body of Jesus would have been stretched to its fullest, with enormous pain coming from His feet and hands. This, however, was merciful compared to what happened next.

Once Jesus was firmly attached to the cross, then several strong soldiers lifted up the cross from off the ground and carried it to a spot where there was a *four-to-five-foot deep* hole in the ground. This hole was the perfect size for the long standing beam of the cross to slip into; this hole is what supported the weight of the cross and the prisoner on it. The soldiers lined up the cross and then dropped it into the hole, cut into the rock formations on the hill. This four to five-foot free-fall drop probably dislocated every one of Jesus' bones from its joints when the cross hit the bottom. *"I am poured out like water, and all my bones are out of joint" (Psalm 22:14).* You can imagine what grueling pain this must have caused. The continual hanging on the cross from this point on caused the body to cramp up and contort violently due to lack of oxygen and blood to certain muscles of the body. It would have been very difficult to breathe while hanging with the weight of His body on His hands, so in order to breathe, Jesus would have had to muster the strength to lift His body up by putting all His weight on His feet firmly held by that steel spike. This would have caused excruciating pain but would have allowed Him to breathe. After enduring this for several hours, Jesus died and gave up the ghost. Remember what the prophet said concerning Jesus, *"As many were astonied at thee; his visage was so marred more than any man, and his form more than the sons of men"* (Isaiah 52:14). Jesus endured what no man could because He loved us. He preferred going through that horrible death rather than to see you and me perish forever in eternal damnation.

I highly encourage you to read *Psalm 22* and *Isaiah 53* in order to better understand the suffering that Jesus paid for you and me. The first 21 verses of *Psalm 22* pertain to the crucifixion; they are written from the perspective of Christ hanging from the cross. Verse 22 onward deals with the resurrection. *Isaiah 53* deals with Jesus' suffering, why it was necessary, and how it satisfied God's holy nature. Read them carefully so that you can better appreciate what Jesus did for you and me; each is short. Remember, Jesus died as a sin offering, a sacrifice, on our behalf. God was bruising Him because He bore our sins and paid the price for them all, and this sacrifice was sufficient to fully satisfy God. (See *Isaiah 53:10-11.*) That is why John the Baptist called Jesus the Lamb of God; He was going to be that Lamb that laid down His life for you and me. Praise God for that!

CHAPTER 9

Israel—The Firstborn of God

On January 31, 1933, Adolf Hitler took power in the highest echelons of the German government, along with his Nazi party. He had long before laid out his platform and his plans in his manifesto, *Mein Kampf.* Shortly after taking power, Hitler assembled his staff to address "the Jewish Question"; this was the terminology used by Hitler to address his devilish plans to eliminate the Jewish people from Germany. Hitler and the Nazi party would not tolerate the Jewish presence in Germany and blamed them for all the ills of their society. Never mind that no evidence existed linking the Jewish people with these societal problems because, in Hitler's warped mind, the Jews were to blame for all of society's problems. For this reason, "the Jewish Question" and its ultimate solution was of supreme importance to Hitler.

The result of these meetings paved the framework leading to the final solution to this problem; Hitler's government would create several concentration camps whose chief function was to exterminate human life. According to the plan, the Jewish people would be removed from their homes into Jewish ghettos until they could be transported by railway to these concentration camps. Once the camps were ready, the Jews were forcefully herded like cattle into railway cars without any amenities, where they remained until they arrived at the concentration camp. Once there, the German officers and staff carried out efficient and mass extermination. The killings were brutal and without mercy, and according to historians, over six million Jews were executed in these death camps. But the Nazis were not the first to target the Jews. History is replete with rulers who sought to exterminate the Israelites. From Pharaoh in *Exodus 1* to the narcissist Haman who ruled in the Persian empire as found in the book of *Esther*, to the persecution of the dark ages, the Israelites have been despised by society for thousands of years. But why? How can this little race of people draw so much attention and hatred? Furthermore, is it acceptable as a Christian to take such a position against the Jewish people and still be in favor with God? We will explore the answers to these questions in this chapter.

Before we address the questions raised above, I think it important to understand the history of how the Jewish people came into existence. After the Jews were in bondage in Egypt and were suffering at the hands of Pharaoh, God told Moses to speak unto Pharaoh and say, *"Thus saith the LORD, Israel is my son, even my first-born" (Exodus 4:22).* But how could God say this? Israel wasn't born until Isaac begat Jacob, over two thousand years after God created Adam in the Garden of Eden. Adam clearly was not a Jew; otherwise, all of his off-spring would have been Jewish, too. The nations, such as the people of Mesopotamia, the Egyptian empire, and all the others, were born out of Adam's offspring, but none of these nations were Jewish. The Jewish nation was born out of Jacob, whom God later named Israel af-ter he took all of his family (seventy persons) into Egypt during a crippling famine. (*Genesis 46:27; Deuteronomy 10:22.*) God said that He chose Israel over the other na-tions, not because they were great in numbers (for they were but a few), but because God loved them and would keep the oath He had sworn to their fathers (Abraham, Isaac, and Jacob). (See *Deuteronomy 7:7-8.*) "Aha! You just said that the Jewish people weren't born until Ja-cob's birth, but Jacob's father and grandfather had to be Jewish. How else could Jacob be Jewish?" That is a good question. Let me explain. God told Abraham, *"As for me, behold, my covenant is with thee, and thou shalt be a father of many nations" (Genesis 17:4).* God kept His word, and to-day Abraham is considered the father of many nations. That being the case, he couldn't have been purely Jewish. Abraham's son of promise was Isaac, who himself bore two sons, Esau and Jacob. Esau is the father of the Edomite people, who come from modern-day Jordan. They also are not Jewish. Jacob, however, was the one through whom God would fulfill His promises to Abraham; his sons and their descendants are the Jewish people we know today.

So if the Jewish race did not come into existence until Jacob's birth, how could God truly say that Israel is His firstborn, as Moses told Pharaoh? In scripture, "firstborn" does not necessarily mean "born first." In the ancient traditions, the firstborn was the beginning of the strength of the father, and he was entitled to a position of honor where he would inherit a double portion compared to his brothers. (See *Deuteronomy 21:17*.) Thus, the firstborn was the son who inherited this coveted double portion and who held the position of honor in the family. When God calls Israel His firstborn, He is not saying that the nation of Israel was born first before all other nations; He is saying that Israel holds the position of honor amongst the nations, and they would inherit a double portion of God's blessings. It's a position of prestige and honor before Almighty God that other nations simply do not hold. It was through the Jewish nation that God would raise up the Messiah who would take on the sins of the world to bring many sons to glory; it was through the Jewish nation that the Messiah would deliver the fatal blow to Satan and death; it was to the Jewish nation that God would commit the oracles of God as Paul stated in *Romans 3:2*; it was through the Jewish nation that God would transmit His word to the world and have it preserved for all generations; it was through the Jewish nation that God would launch the fame of His name throughout the world (as seen in the Exodus...and He will do it again as outlined in *Ezekiel 38-39!*). Much has God given the world through the nation of Israel, and God will always love them.

It is because of God's use of Israel in bringing forth Jesus and God's word that the devil absolutely hates Israel. He has moved kings and armies to plot against, scheme against, and attack the Jewish people in the hopes of wiping them off the face of the earth. This has been happening for centuries upon centuries, and Jewish people have found themselves the objects of persecution, scorn, and fear. Plot after plot has been laid, but none has ever been successful in exterminating the Jewish people, and no such plot ever will be. "Why not?" you ask. Because God must protect them in keeping with His word. Many nations out of ancient history no longer exist, such as the Philistines, the Ammonites, the Hittites, the Jebusites, and numerous others. Israel was a contemporary of these and was targeted by many nations, yet the Jewish people continue to survive and thrive. The reason is God's supernatural protection. *"Behold, the eyes of the Lord GOD are upon the sinful king-*

dom, and I will destroy it from off the face of the earth; saving that I will not utterly destroy the house of Jacob, saith the LORD" (Amos 9:8).

> And yet for all that [in this particular passage, God has just pronounced that severe judgment would come against the Jewish people for their disobedience], when they be in the land of their enemies, I will not cast them away, neither will I abhor them, to destroy them utterly, and to break my covenant with them: for I am the LORD their God.
>
> *Leviticus 26:44* (brackets added for clarity)

God states very clearly that He will never allow Israel to be destroyed, though many have surely tried!

It is clear that God still loves Israel and will be faithful to them because His word declares it. But God also will perform this task of guarding Israel for His name's sake. Hear God's own words:

> Therefore say unto the house of Israel, thus saith the Lord GOD; I do not this for your sakes, O house of Israel, but for mine holy name's sake, which ye have profaned among the heathen, whither ye went.
>
> *Ezekiel 36:22*

God said of his people Israel, *"The LORD hath appeared of old unto me, saying, Yea, I have loved thee with an everlasting love: therefore with lovingkindness have I drawn thee"* (Jeremiah 31:2). So if God loves and protects Israel, can any of us be justified before God for hating and despising them? No, we can't. It would be the ultimate hypocrisy for a person to say they love God and are in good standing with Him but despise the Jewish people. First, we are told in the Bible that we are to love even our enemies. So we can never be justified before God in despising and hating any people. But second, God says we are liars if we claim to love God and hate the Jew. *"If a man say, I love God, and hateth his brother, he is a liar: for he that loveth not his brother whom he hath seen, how can he love God whom he hath not seen?"* (1 John 4:20)

Still, there are many reasons people raise when trying to justify their hatred of the Jews, such as "they killed Jesus" or "they rejected Jesus so God rejected them" or "God divorced the Jews, and the church has taken its place and its promises," and many others. All such statements are ungodly and without support in the scriptures. For example, the "they killed Jesus" claim is baseless. Historically speaking, the Jewish leaders delivered Jesus to Pontius Pilate, and the Romans put Jesus to death. But even more to the point, it was God who made sure it all happened. "What!" you say! *"That* is blasphemy!" Hold on...let God speak.

> Yet it pleased the LORD to bruise him [Jesus]; he hath put him to grief: when thou shalt make his soul an offering for sin, he shall see his seed, he shall prolong his days, and the pleasure of the LORD shall prosper in his hand. He shall see of the travail of his soul, and shall be satisfied: by his knowledge shall my righteous servant justify many; for he shall bear their iniquities.
>
> *Isaiah 53:10-11*

Here we can see that God the Father was pleased to bruise Jesus and that God put Him to grief, ultimately making an offering of Jesus' soul for the iniquities of humanity. Jesus Himself, while praying at the Garden of Gethsemane, prayed that God would take the cup (the suffering and death of the cross) away from Him. But, he also prayed that God's will would be done. (See *Mark* 14:34-36.) One last thought, although there are others...Jesus Himself also said

> Therefore doth my Father love me, because I lay down my life, that I might take it again. No man taketh it from me, but I lay it down of myself. I have power to lay it down, and I

have power to take it again. This commandment have I received of my Father.

John 10:17-18

So, Jesus went to die on purpose of His own will,
and no man, Jew or otherwise, took it from Him. So the
Jews did not kill Jesus; He offered Himself to save us.

Each justification raised to hate or oppose the Jewish people is equally refuted by scripture. Thus, it is in-
consistent with the heart of God, who loves the Jewish
people, to be a born-again believer bound for heaven
because of the sacrifice of Jesus and have hatred or in-
difference for the Jews. Don't forget, Jesus was a full-
blooded Jew. Lastly, God has plans for Israel that include exercising the rights of the firstborn: *"That they
[Israel] may possess the remnant of Edom, and of all the
heathen, which are called by my name, saith the LORD that
doeth this"* (Amos 9:12) *(brackets added for clarity)*. According to this passage, God will ultimately make the Jewish people the head of the nations. This is precisely in
keeping with the rights and privileges of the "firstborn
among the nations," as God has described them. So we
should love, bless, and encourage our Jewish friends.
We should also *"Pray for the peace of Jerusalem: they shall
prosper that love thee"* (Psalm 122:6).

CHAPTER 10

What is Love, Really?

Probably the most misused and misunderstood word in the English language is the word "love." Its everyday meaning spans an enormous area and applies to everything from grandmothers to sporting events to pizza. How often have you heard something like, "What did you think about the new movie?" "I just loved it!" Christians are called to love; it is probably the major characteristic that defines the Christian life. But what exactly does it really mean? How are we supposed to "love our neighbors" or anything like that if we don't really understand what God is commanding us to do? It's a fair and important question that deserves an answer.

Our society has come to consider "love" as synonymous with a strong feeling or desire associated with pleasure. Poets, songwriters, and others have paved the way for this concept to take root. *Are You Lonesome Tonight?* The number one hit by Elvis Presley in the 1950s exemplifies this truth. In the lyrics, the writer says, "I loved you at first glance." A more modern tune states, "Baby, is this love for real?...let me in your arms to feel." There are many other examples where love is known or gauged by the intensity of the feeling stirred inside of them. Can this be what God refers to when talking about love? Absolutely not.

In *Romans 5:8*, it states, *"But God commendeth [demonstrates] his love toward us, in that, while we were yet sinners, Christ died for us"* (brackets added for clarity). God demonstrated His love for humanity by sending Jesus to sacrifice Himself for us, and He did so while humanity was in total rebellion against God. There wasn't anybody looking to please God or serve God or seek God; everybody was doing his or her own thing and pursuing his or her own interests. As the Bible says,

> As it is written, There is none righteous, no, not one: There is none that understandeth, there is none that seeketh after God. They are all gone out of the way, they are together become unprofitable; there is none that doeth good, no, not one.
>
> *Romans 3:10-12*

The Bible also says that God spoke, saying, *"And I sought for a man among them, that should make up the hedge, and stand in the gap before me for the land, that I should not destroy it: but I found none" (Ezekiel 22:30)*. Yet, even though nobody was seeking after the things of God, God "loved" them anyway. But does this mean that God had strong, intense feelings of pleasure toward humanity, and this stirred God to act as He did? No.

In the Bible, "love" is used as a verb, a term of action. For example, Jesus said that His followers are to "love your enemies." Notice that the word is used as a verb, something we are to do. If feelings were the foundation for biblical love, then how could we ever comply with this commandment? Enemies are, by definition, people who are actively opposed or hostile to us. How many of you have deep, strong feelings of pleasure toward these types of people? Whatever strong feelings we typically have about our enemies are generally those of disgust, contempt, and hatred. Therefore, it stands to reason that it is not possible that feelings can form the basis of Jesus' command to love our enemies. There has to be something deeper that we are missing.

In *1 Corinthians 13*, God has actually defined "love" for us. Here is what the Bible says:

> Though I speak with the tongues of men and of angels, and have not charity [love], I am become as sounding brass, or a tinkling cymbal. And though I have the gift of prophecy, and

understand all mysteries, and all knowledge; and though I have all faith, so that I could remove mountains, and have not charity, I am nothing. And though I bestow all my goods to feed the poor, and though I give my body to be burned, and have not charity, it profiteth me nothing. [Now the definition begins] Charity suffereth long, and is kind; charity envieth not; charity vaunteth not itself, is not puffed up, Doth not behave itself unseemly, seeketh not her own, is not easily provoked, thinketh no evil; Rejoiceth not in iniquity, but rejoiceth in the truth; Beareth all things, believeth all things, hopeth all things, endureth all things.

1 Corinthians 13:1-7
(brackets added for clarity)

Let us look at this passage a little more carefully, for it is here that God has provided us with His concept of "love." First of all, notice in the first portion of this text that if the foundation or the reason for the good works is anything but love, that good work has no value to God. There are many people who have led church services, donated lots of time or money (or both), worked with the poor or underprivileged, and many other such things, but they did so for reasons other than love. All of those works profit nothing. I, myself, have taught and preached the Bible for well over twenty years (as of the writing of this book), and I have served in political office, too. If I did the teaching and preaching for the purpose of getting myself known in the community, for the purpose of someday getting votes, or for the purpose of making my business more profitable, then all of my work will have been for nothing when I stand before God. The reason that I should be doing these works is that I love people, I love God, and I am seeking to be obedient to Him. There is a passage in *Matthew 7* where certain people are cast away into hell, and they protest, reminding God that they did lots of good works while they lived. (See *Matthew 7:21-23*.) Those works, however, were not motivated by love but by something else.

Back to our passage: God begins the definition in verse 4. He says that love suffers long, or in other words, it is patient. Here we are told that true love acts with patience towards the object of that love. This means that when my spouse or child or neighbor does something that really upsets me or annoys me, I am called to treat them with patience. This reminds me of being around a mentally incapacitated person who doesn't understand the world in the same way as you or me. When they constantly jerk, make verbal outbursts, or anything similar, we don't yell at them or punish them. We act with patience because we understand their condition and their inability to harness it. God calls us all to act with that same kind of patience towards everybody! He says that is a characteristic of true love. Then the definition continues by stating that love is kind. This means that we are not only to be patient towards others, we are to be kind too. This is the same type of kindness that we routinely show towards strangers we meet or the boss' spouse or your soon-to-be in-laws. We go out of our way to be nice, friendly, and helpful. This is exactly what God says true love looks like.

The definition changes form after this because God is trying to make it clear to us the essence of His concept of love. Have you ever tried to define for your child what "warm" means? How would you do that? Most of us would say something like, "Warm is when it is not too hot and not too cold; it is somewhere in the middle and slightly closer to hot than cold." This is fairly normal and about the best we could do when trying to explain this concept to a child. God does the exact same thing when trying to explain to us the concept of love. After telling us two things that form the basis of love, He then turns to tell us what love is not. He says that love does not act in a way that vaunts itself or is puffed up. This means that we don't bring glory and attention to ourselves (vaunting ourselves), and we don't act proud, as if we are better than people around us (puffed up). When we act in these ways, we turn the focus away from the person we are dealing with, and we turn it back to ourselves; God says that is not love. So if we are to love God's way, we will be humble and lift up the people around us.

The definition continues by stating that love does not behave itself unseemly and doesn't seek its own. In other words, love is not rude and is not motivated by trying to do something for ourselves. Many of us are really rude when dealing with other people, especially those closest to us, and we try to justify it by something like, "well, they deserve it" or "that is just the way I am, and they know that" or some other justification. God says we are to love, and when we love, we cannot be rude. We are also to act towards others in a way that ultimately is not designed to help ourselves. There are many ways this is demonstrated, including speaking with flattery (which is done so the other person will like you), helping others with the expectation or hope that something good will come back to you, and other such things where the end result is your benefit. Paul loved the Jewish people so much that he said he wished he could be accursed of God if it meant they could be saved (*Romans 9:3*). This is classic and true love. If Paul could have gotten his wish, what benefit could he have expected for himself? Absolutely none. He would be forever in hell. True love is never rude to the people we are interacting with, and true love never seeks out our own advancement.

The definition then continues by stating that love is not easily provoked, and it thinks no evil. In other words, it takes a lot of poor behavior from the person we are interacting with before we lose our cool and get angry. When it says that it thinks no evil, it means that we don't assume the worst in the person we are interacting with; we don't jump to conclusions without having a solid factual basis (gossip, rumors, and "because I just know" are not a solid factual basis). We give the person the benefit of the doubt until it is firmly established through facts of that person's wrong.

God then says love doesn't rejoice in sin but rejoices in the truth. I wish our society would grasp this. How many shows are on television where sin is openly flaunted, and we don't condemn it and aren't offended by it; instead, we cheer. You are not acting in love when you cheer and encourage sin, but you do act in love when you rest and rejoice in the word of God and in things that are just, godly, and pure. After all, it is the words of God that are able to make thee wise unto salvation (2 *Timothy 3:15*). This means that we are to delight in the truth because it is the only way the person we are interacting with can see God.

Lastly, God says love bears all things. That means it can take anything others throw at us. Love believes and hopes all things, meaning we believe all the truths God has laid out for us in the Bible, and we pass those along to others in our words and actions. Love endures all things, meaning we continue to love others even when things are not working well for us.

So what is the common thread throughout the entire definition God has provided us? Choice and sacrifice. Those are the common thread. When we are patient and kind, it is a choice we must make for the good of the other person. When we don't look to benefit ourselves, when we don't assume the worst, and when we endure all things, those are all choices we make; they are all for the good of the other person. Love, then, from God's perspective, is being selfless and acting in a way that will bless and benefit the person with whom you are dealing. There is no room for our feelings to demonstrate our love; our love is a choice that glorifies God.

Imagine how our marriages and other relationships would be totally transformed if both persons lived in this way? Divorces and broken families would be a thing of the past. Feelings come, and feelings go; our moods change due to chemical variations in our bodies or due to the circumstances we are living with at the time. If love is based on a feeling, then that love is subject to being lost, and it often happens rather quickly. If love is based on choice and sacrifice for the other person, we can love even our enemies and show the world what God is like!

CHAPTER 11

The Rapture of the Church...a Real Event or an Imaginary Concept?

Growing up in deep south Texas in a predominantly Roman Catholic population (of which I was one), there was very little Bible study in most homes. One doctrine, however, that I had "learned" about was that of the Rapture of the Church; the idea that Jesus was going to come at any minute and take His people out of this world. One of the most successful book series ever written was *Left Behind*, about the people who were left on planet earth after Jesus came and removed His people and the difficulties that they endured during the Great Tribulation period. Does the Bible actually support such a doctrine, and if so, what does it mean for us? Or is this only an imaginary concept?

Paul outlined the prophecy of believers meeting the Lord "in the air," being snatched out of this world when he wrote:

> But I would not have you ignorant, brethren, concerning them which are asleep [dead], that ye sorrow not, even as others which have no hope. For if we believe that Jesus died and rose again, even so them also which sleep in Jesus will God bring with him. For this we say unto you by the word of the Lord, that we which are alive and remain unto the coming of the Lord shall not prevent them which are asleep. For the Lord himself shall descend from heaven with a shout, with the voice of the archangel, and with the trump of God: and the dead in Christ shall rise first: then we which are alive and remain shall be caught up together with them in the clouds, to meet the Lord in the air: and so shall we ever be with the Lord. Wherefore comfort one another with these words.
>
> *1 Thessalonians 4:13-18*
> (brackets added for clarity)

This passage forms the basis of the doctrine, and it is not found anywhere else in the entire Bible. Let us examine it more closely to dig out the major nuggets of truth.

First of all, Paul wrote these words to comfort and assure the Thessalonian believers that Jesus had not yet returned. These believers had been told that Jesus had already returned, and they were left dazed, confused, and wondering how they could have missed it all. They also questioned what was to happen to those who had already died, believing that Jesus was the Messiah but never seeing the fulfillment of the promises. All seemed lost to these confused believers. Paul addressed the matter by providing the information in our passage. Paul provided comfort by assuring them that those who had already died believing in Jesus would be raised from the dead at Jesus' return, and they would be with Jesus forevermore. "For if we believe that Jesus died and rose again, even so them also which sleep in Jesus will God bring with him." So, the dead were not lost or forgotten; they were going to be with Jesus, too, when He returns.

Next, the passage turns to those who are still alive: "For this we say unto you by the word of the Lord, that we which are alive and remain unto the coming of the Lord shall not prevent them which are asleep. For the Lord himself shall descend from heaven with a shout, with the voice of the archangel, and with the trump of God: and the dead in Christ shall rise first." Here, Paul states that those believers who are alive when Jesus returns will not "prevent" those who are dead. "Prevent" is the old English word for "precede" or "go before." In other words, the living will not go before those who have already died when Jesus returns. "'Go before' what?" you may ask. Look at the first part of the next sentence: Jesus will return by descending from heaven with a "shout" and the "voice of the archangel" and with "the trump of God," and the dead in Christ *shall rise first!* When Jesus returns, it will be obvious to all believers (and maybe the world...the Bible isn't clear on that point) because He will descend with much fanfare, a shout, the voice of the archangel, and the trump of God. When that happens, Paul says, those who died believing and hoping in Jesus will be the raised from the dead and shall rise up to Jesus as the first ones in line to meet Jesus face to face. The living will not go before them.

"Well, what about those who are living...what happens to them?" you may be asking. Look at the rest of the sentence: "and the dead in Christ shall rise first: then we which are alive and remain shall be caught up together with them in the clouds, to meet the Lord in the air: and so shall we ever be with the Lord." It is clear from this passage that the living will be "caught up" together with them (the dead who were raised first) in the clouds to meet Jesus in the air; a grand reunion of all believers from ages past to the present. A few things here: the Greek word translated into "caught up" is the word *harpazo*. That word means "to seize" or "to catch away" or "to snatch." The believers who are alive will be "snatched" off the earth by God. "What does that mean?" I hear you saying. Let me illustrate. There was a popular children's game when I was a boy in the late 1960s and early 1970s called "Jacks." "Jacks" was a very simple game to learn, but it took practice and coordination to get good at it. In this game, a small rubber ball and about ten small metal objects called "jacks" were needed (the jacks were basically three individual half-inch long rods that all joined together in their centers and facing out, away from each other, like a three-dimensional grid). To play, the jacks were dropped randomly on the floor. The player would allow the rubber ball to drop to the floor while kneeling, and before the ball could bounce twice, the player had to grab one jack off the floor and catch the ball in the same hand. If successful, he would drop the ball a second time, and he had to grab two jacks off the floor before the ball bounced twice. This would continue, each time grabbing an additional jack until the player was unsuccessful. In the game, the jacks would be *harpazo* or snatched up. This is the truth taught in this passage. God will seize all believers when He returns, and they will immediately be gone from this planet. Their destination is high in the atmosphere where Jesus will be waiting for them; then, it's off to heaven to be with Jesus forevermore. These are words of comfort and encouragement to the believers since it makes it clear what our future holds. "How long is this going to take? It seems like a pretty lengthy and difficult process," you say. Remember, God has unlimited power, and this task will be supremely easy for Him. We are told in the Bible that this will all happen *"in a moment, in the twinkling of an eye"* (1 Corinthians 15:52). That is a fraction of a second!

"But wait a minute. I thought dead believers automatically went to heaven to be with Jesus the moment they died. Isn't that what the Bible teaches? I heard that somewhere. If that is true, then why are they now meeting Jesus again at some time in the future to go back to heaven again? This doesn't make any sense." That is an outstanding question. You are correct. The Bible clearly teaches that when a believer dies, he is immediately present with Jesus, who sits on God's right hand in heaven. (See *2 Corinthians 5:6-8* and *Psalm 110:1*.) At the moment of death in our world, the spirit of an individual is separated from that individual's body. The body cannot live without the spirit (see *James 2:26*), and once they separate, death is immediate. At that point, the believer's spirit goes immediately to be present with Jesus, but the body doesn't make that journey. The body goes into the grave to return to dust. Thus, in heaven today are the souls of believers from days gone by, but they don't have bodies yet. You get a glimpse of this concept in *Revelation 6:9*, where we read, *"And when he had opened the fifth seal, I saw under the altar the souls of them that were slain for the word of God, and for the testimony which they held."* These people existed as "souls under the altar," yet they were in heaven. It's at the time of the Rapture that we will have our old, corruptible, decayed bodies immediately changed into glorious bodies like that of Jesus Himself, and our souls will reunite with these glorified bodies! Sound too good to be true? Read.

> But some man will say, How are the dead raised up? and with what body do they come? Thou fool, that which thou sowest is not quickened, except it die: and that which thou sowest, thou sowest not that body that shall be, but bare grain, it may chance of wheat, or of some other grain: but God giveth it a body as it hath pleased him, and to every seed his own body. All flesh is not the same flesh: but there is one kind of flesh of men, another flesh of beasts, another of fishes, and another of birds. There are also celestial bodies, and bodies terrestrial: but the glory of the celestial is one, and the glory of the terrestrial is another. There is one glory of the sun, and another glory of the moon, and another glory of

the stars: for one star differeth from another star in glory. So also is the resurrection of the dead. It is sown in corruption; it is raised in incorruption: It is sown in dishonour: it is raised in glory: it is sown in weakness; it is raised in power: it is sown a natural body; it is raised a spiritual body. There is a natural body, and there is a spiritual body.

Now this I say, brethren, that flesh and blood cannot inherit the kingdom of God; neither doth corruption inherit incorruption. Behold, I shew you a mystery; We shall not all sleep [die], but we shall all be changed, in a moment, in the twinkling of an eye, at the last trump: for the trumpet shall sound, and the dead shall be raised incorruptible, and we shall be changed. For this corruptible must put on incorruption, and this mortal must put on immortality.

1 Corinthians 15:35-44; 50-53
(brackets added for clarity)

Let's try to break down the basics of this section of scripture. You can see that the believers in Corinth were having trouble understanding how a dead person could be raised up again, and even if they could be, they couldn't grasp what kind of bodies they could possibly be. The bodies of the dead were decayed and worm-eaten. In some cases, there was nothing left of the body since many early Christians were killed and eaten by animals in the Roman Colosseum; others would have been lost to fires or drowned and decomposed at sea. But for God, the task of putting together a body is a trivial one. Paul addresses the issue by using farming principles they could all understand to illustrate his point. He reminded them that when you plant seed, the seed must first die before it will sprout up. If the seed doesn't die, it won't sprout up. Jesus Himself said the same thing when He said, *"Verily, verily, I say unto you, Except a corn of wheat fall into the ground and die, it abideth alone: but if it die, it bringeth forth much fruit"* (John 12:24). Then Paul continues by telling them that the farmer plants seed in the ground, not the final, mature vine or bush or tree that will ultimately sprout up. The seed goes in the ground, but when the seed sprouts, it sprouts looking totally different than the seed that was put into the ground; it has totally transformed. It now may have vines, leaves, branches, fruit, etc., whereas the seed that was planted was very small with no such features. Then he tells the readers that there are different kinds of bodies that God has made; bodies for plants, birds, fishes, man, etc. Then he says there is a natural body (the one we are all familiar with), and there is a celestrial body; this celestrial body is the one we will be getting at the time of the Rapture of the church. This is the incorruptible body that we will be given. Paul stated that our old bodies are "sown" (planted in the grave) in corruption (they are bodies given to decay, sickness, and sin), but they will be raised looking and being totally different. The new bodies will be immortal and incorruptible, and notice that it will happen in the twinkling of an eye. Fast! Jesus has such a body already. He was seen of the apostles and many of his disciples after his death and resurrection; he appeared and disappeared; he passed through walls and entered rooms with locked doors. We will have bodies that function just like His! John the apostle wrote, "Beloved, now are we the sons of God, and it doth not yet appear what we shall be: but we know that, when he shall appear, we shall be like him; for we shall see him as he is" (1 John 3:2). Did you see it? John said we don't know yet what we are going to be like, but we do know that when He comes again (the Rapture we have been studying), we shall be like Him and see Him as He is. This is how we know that we will be given bodies that are like His body. Now please don't hear what I clearly did not say. We are not going to be gods, but we are going to be given bodies that are like His body. Can you imagine that! No wonder the Bible says, "But as it is written, Eye hath not seen, nor ear heard, neither have entered into the heart of man, the things which God hath prepared for them that love him" (*1 Corinthians 2:9*).

"That sounds fantastic, but when is all this supposed to happen?" you ask. As you can see from the initial passage in 1 Thessalonians 4 that we first saw above, Paul was expecting it at any moment. He said, "the dead in Christ shall rise first: then we which are alive..." Paul included himself in the group of those who were alive looking for Jesus to return. He could have written, "then those who will be alive," meaning that he would have known the return would have been after his death. But Paul didn't know, and nobody knows when Jesus will return. Jesus Himself said, *"But of that day and hour knoweth no man, no, not the angels of heaven, but my Father only" (Matthew 24:36).* He also said, *"Watch therefore: for ye know not what hour your Lord doth come" (Matthew 24:42).* The Rapture of the church can happen at any moment, and when God has arrived at the date circled on His heavenly calendar (and with each passing day, we get one day closer), then Jesus will stand up and snatch up His church out of the world. Everybody else will be left behind. Will you be snatched away, or will you be left behind? Jesus can come at any moment...are you ready?

CHAPTER 12

Why So Many Religions?

In the movie *Indiana Jones and the Last Crusade,* our hero is desperately trying to find the Holy Grail, the cup which Jesus used during the last supper with His disciples, in order to save the life of his father. His search ends in a large room that is filled with hundreds of cups, all of different shapes, sizes, colors, and designs. In the movie, one of them is the actual Holy Grail, and all the others are frauds. If the hero is able to successfully find the actual cup Jesus used, then drinking from the contents would bring eternal life, thus saving the life of his dying father. If, however, he chooses the wrong cup, then the drink would lead to certain and immediate death. As made clear in the movie, the only way for our hero to determine if the right choice was made was to take a drink. Once the drink was taken, the choice was made and could not be undone, and the consequences to follow were certain, whether good or bad. What a clever way to conceal the true identity of the actual grail and protect it from ever being found, by hiding it in plain sight surrounded by hundreds of fakes. The tactics of the devil are even more clever. But unlike the movies, which are made for entertainment, the devil plays for blood.

In our society, there are many religions where people can learn about spiritual things, find company and friendship with others, and obtain purpose and direction for their lives. Religion gives people a sense of belonging and meaning in their lives. In their religion, they find comfort, confirmation deep inside that they are on the right track to God, and ultimately a sense of peace. So why are there so many different religions, and does it matter which one you choose to embrace?

We have already seen in previous chapters that Jesus was born so that He could die on the cross for the sins of man. Jesus taught, *"I am the way, the truth, and the life: no man cometh unto the Father, but by me"* (John 14:6). The path to God must come through Jesus; there is no other way. Yet, in the Bible, we find that we have an enemy whose deepest desire is to destroy us all! The Bible tells us: *"Be sober, be vigilant; because your adversary the devil, as a roaring lion, walketh about, seeking whom he may devour"* (1 Peter 5:8). The devil is not a part of some fairy tale, nor is he the figment of somebody's imagination. The Bible is absolutely clear that the devil is an evil being who is hunting for your soul! "Come on, man! Stop trying to scare me. How could some devil possibly do that?" you may be saying. The devil does this by employing very skilled and clever deceptions, distractions, and misdirection. And he is very good at it!

Before God created man and the earth, as found in *Genesis 1*, He had already created the angelic host as seen in *Job 38:6-7*. Among those created angelic beings was a particularly radiant angel named Lucifer, who would later become Satan. While in heaven, Lucifer led a rebellion against God. Stop for a moment to think about this. These angels lived in heaven with God; a perfect paradise where was no sin. Even in these perfect surroundings and in the actual presence of God Himself, Lucifer was so good at deceiving that he was able to get one-third of the angels to rebel against God and follow him. I have always found that an absolutely staggering fact. If Satan is good enough to deceive the angels who were living with God in heaven to rebel against God, then he is a master at his trade, and I suspect the human soul is much easier prey than the angels.

From the beginning of man's history, the devil has been engaged in leading people away from God and the truth. It all began in the Garden of Eden. There were only two people living on this planet that was full of goodness and the abundance of God. After God had given instructions to Adam, He (God) set them in the middle of the Garden. They both knew what God had said; there was no misunderstanding. Then the devil came along and found Eve, where he commenced his attack. Not with a sword or a club did he attack her. He did it with sneaky deception. He began by challenging the truth of what God had told them. (There are many people down through the centuries and among us today who also challenge the truth of God's word, the Holy Bible. They do not realize that by doing so; they are doing the devil's bidding by following in his exact footprints left in the Garden of Eden.) He said that God was keeping things from them and implied that God didn't have their best interests at heart. After this exchange, Eve believed the devil over God. Just like those angels that rebelled, she chose to reject what God had said and believe the devil, and as a result, she sinned by taking and eating the forbidden fruit. There is no indication in the Bible that Adam was present when this attack occurred, but when Eve brought the fruit to Adam, Adam chose to eat of the fruit, knowing that it was forbidden, and man was now lost. The devil had succeeded in destroying their blissful existence. Now, if that is where the story ended, then these two would have surely been forever lost. But God intervened and provided a way to save them, much to the disgust of the devil! Adam and Eve, just like everybody else, would have to be saved by believing in the future work of one in the line of their offspring, Jesus.

From that time forward, the devil began working hard to lead mankind away from the truth about the coming Savior that God had promised in *Genesis 3:15*. Soon, Cain (the oldest child of Adam and Eve) was bringing sacrifices to God that were contrary to what God required. Cain wanted to approach God in his way, not God's way, and God condemned it as sin. (See *Genesis 4:1-7*.) As time passed, the population exploded, and many people were living on the earth, and new "religions" began to arise. There were people who began worshipping the sun, moon, and stars; others began worshipping gods they believed were unique to them; and some began to worship other people as gods (such as the worship of Nimrod in the days of the Tower of Babel). Early in man's history, because of Adam's fall, there was already much corruption, deceit, and ultimately sin in the world. Do we have to wonder where Cain got his idea and where the rest of the human population would later get their ideas? No. They were seduced and deceived by the devil. When speaking of the devil in one passage, the Bible states that the devil is to be cast into the bottomless pit and be sealed there for a time, *"that he should deceive the nations no more"* (*Revelation 20:3*). It also states: *"How art thou fallen from heaven, O Lucifer, son of the morning! how art thou cut down to the ground, which didst weaken the nations!" (Isaiah 14:12)* The word "weaken" here is the Hebrew word *chalash* which means to overthrow, to decay, or to waste away. This is the devil's work on this earth; it is to deceive people and lead them away from God and His salvation through Jesus, causing them to be overthrown or to decay (spiritually, of course).

Over the centuries, the devil has moved men to commence new religions that appeal to different portions of humanity. Most of these have no reference to Jesus at all, only to a God. Most of these have a path laid before men, which must be followed to attain God, the path typically being constructed of the good works of men. Even in these religions which don't speak of Jesus, men find satisfaction, and often, a sense of peace. If a man finds satisfaction and peace, why would he ever look elsewhere? Some of these religions recognize Jesus and His claims to being God's Son, but they don't recognize Jesus as God. Most of these religious followers also have some aspect of their salvation dependent on works which they must do. Hundreds of religions flood our world today, and only one way can save the human soul. Just like the Indiana Jones movie, a person must choose which religion they will embrace, and the only way a person will ultimately discover whether he/she made the right choice is to follow that religion and wait for the results after death. Jesus said,

Enter ye in at the strait gate: for wide is the gate, and broad is the way, that leadeth to destruction, and many there be which go in thereat: Because strait is the gate, and narrow is the way, which leadeth unto life, and few there be that find it.

Matthew 7:13-14

My prayer for you is that you find Jesus because no religion will work!

CHAPTER 13

The Structure of the Family

God is a God of order and structure, not of chaos. This can be seen in nature from the inner workings of the cell to the vast reaches of our ever-expanding universe. While this is clearly seen in nature, it is not always evident in our humanity. Every day we see devastation, violence, war, and chaos in the news. We see the statistical rates climbing for divorces, unwed mothers, single-parent homes, homeless people, juvenile delinquents, drug addiction, and on and on. The family unit is the backbone of any society, and the decline evident in our society can be directly attributable to our failing families. God ordained the family unit, but the human race has chosen to live within the family according to its own terms and has largely ignored God's commandments and direction for the family unit. When the family fails, society is destined to fall, and the evidence is clearly seen in today's daily news. God has order and structure designed for the family, but our "enlightened" society has chosen its own set of rules, and our families are suffering the consequences of those poor choices.

Before you continue reading this chapter, ask yourself the following questions: What kind of family did I grow up in? How did my parents act towards each other and towards us? How did we children act towards our parents and others? Was this different from the family that I formed in my adult life with my spouse? What could I have done differently? What can I do to change things today? While I realize that nobody is able to change the past, it is my hope that with God's blessing and help, we can understand how to make changes to improve the future. The past is etched in stone, but the future is a blank canvas, able to accept any markings we choose to make.

As a child growing up in deep south Texas and in the days when there were no internet or cell phones, I had many friends (and still do today, praise God!). We would meet at the school to play football or meet at somebody's house to do something else. We constantly moved around and got to know almost everybody's parents and siblings. I was struck by the different environments we would encounter in the different homes we visited. Some had overbearing fathers that we all tried to avoid; others had overbearing mothers (we tried to avoid them too). Some of my friends were given very little room to do anything, while others had free reign and did as they pleased. After a little while, we all had a pretty good idea of which houses we wanted to avoid and which were more "kid-friendly." In my young mind, all I had really known was my home and how my parents acted towards each other and towards us children. I thought every home operated the same way but found that was very much not true. Today, I am convinced the variations in the home are even more diverse than when I was a boy since today there are single-parent homes (something almost unheard of in my youth), same-sex marriages (definitely unheard of in my youth), and mixed families (pretty rare, except for Brady Bunch episodes on TV), just to name a few differences. But how is the Christian to live within the family unit? What does the Bible have to say about this important subject? It has much to say, and we had better heed God's commands if we desire peace and blessing for our families.

When God created Adam, He made Adam the overseer of the creation. Adam had fellowship with all living creatures while living in paradise. But God saw that there was not a companion suitable for Adam among the creatures with whom he was living. In fact, the Bible records that God found Adam "alone" in the midst of Eden, surrounded by living creatures of every kind. *"And the LORD God said, It is not good that the man should*

be alone; I will make him an help meet for him" (Genesis 2:18).
There are three things to note about this verse: (1) God
found no suitable companionship for Adam amongst
the creation and said "it is not good"; (2) God charac-
terized this companion He was going to make as "an
help" for Adam; and (3) God described this companion
as "meet" for Adam. Here we see the beginnings of the
family unit that God ordained and created. Notice that
God said the companion was to be "an help" to Adam.
She was created and brought into the family unit to
help Adam. Notice she was not brought in as a "partner"
or a "leader" or a "supervisor" or any other such thing.
God created her as a helper for Adam. We'll discuss this
in a little more detail below. Furthermore, God said she
would be "meet" for Adam. The old English word "meet"
is translated in more modern English as "proper" or
"appropriate." Thus, God said she would be appropriate as a companion for Adam as opposed to any other
creature living in the Garden. The Bible then states that
God performed surgery on Adam by removing one of
his ribs, and from that rib, He created Eve, the first
woman. Now, why would God have created Eve in this
way? He had created Adam out of the dust of the earth,
forming his body with all of its organs, cells, DNA, etc.;
He didn't need a rib or any other body part. Why didn't
He create Eve in the same way? He could have; it would
have been easy. But instead, God chose to remove one

of Adam's ribs to use as the base to create Eve. God wanted Eve to be a part of Adam, not something totally separate from him. The two were destined to become "one flesh," being the first married couple in human history through whom the entire human race would come. Adam immediately saw that she was not like any other creature in God's Garden; she was totally different. She had come from his bone, and he could surely see the similarities. *"And Adam said, This is now bone of my bones, and flesh of my flesh; she shall be called Woman, because she was taken out of Man" (Genesis 2:23).* She was like him in many ways, yet she was also very different. He was masculine, while she was feminine. He was stronger; she was weaker. He was tough; she was tender. He was muscled; she was shapely. He had a deep voice; she had a high-pitched one. He had a square-shaped face; she had a heart-shaped one. He was hairy; she was smooth. God had not made an equivalent person for Adam as Adam had been, but a different kind of person who was clearly part of him. Eve was to come alongside Adam to be his helper, his lover, his friend, his confidant, his counselor, his comforter, and so much more. Adam was surely ecstatic! The Bible goes on to say at this point, *"Therefore shall a man leave his father and his mother, and shall cleave unto his wife: and they shall be one flesh" (Genesis 2:24).* Here, Adam and Eve began their married life together, the only attendees at the wedding being God Himself and the creatures in the Garden.

By providing us with the account of Eve's creation, God has provided the template for the structure and order of the family. Notice in the passage above that God states a man shall "cleave" unto his wife. The word means "to cling to" or "to stick to." The husband is to cling tightly to his wife. This does not mean he is to smother her, but it means he will not let her go; he will stick tightly to her and remain bound to her. When speaking about marriage, Jesus said, *"Wherefore they are no more twain, but one flesh. What therefore God hath joined together, let not man put asunder"* (Matthew 19:6). The man is not to leave his wife through separation, divorce, or abandonment. Instead, he is to cleave unto her and remain alongside her, through good times and bad for as long as they both shall live. This a major problem in our society today. Far too many husbands have abandoned their responsibilities in the family by leaving the home, in direct violation of God's word, and it has caused great problems for all involved. Statistics bear out the impact of this selfish and devilish decision, with children often bearing the brunt of the damage. The man is to love his wife in the same way he loves himself and in the same way Jesus loves His church! Now that is love! Hear the word of God: *"Husbands, love your wives, even as Christ also loved the church, and gave himself for it"* (Ephesians

5:25). *"So ought men to love their wives as their own bodies. He that loveth his wife loveth himself"* (Ephesians 5:28). So if men love their wives in the same way that they love themselves, or with even deeper love, as Jesus loves His church, then it will be impossible for them to leave their wives and their families, but instead, they will labor for them, treasure them, and love them through thick and thin. But all too many men love themselves and their pleasures more than they love their wives and families; this is sin because it violates God's word, and it leaves a trail of devastation for all in the home.

We have already seen how that God created Eve to be an appropriate helper for Adam. What does this mean in our families? Are the two supposed to be equal partners or something else? Paul wrote, *"But I would have you know, that the head of every man is Christ; and the head of the woman is the man; and the head of Christ is God"* (1 Corinthians 11:3). We all understand the concept of "the head" in relation to our bodies. It is the place from which the body is led since from it originate thoughts, ideas, signals, and impulses that drive the body to action; without the head, the body has no function, no purpose, and no life. This is the concept Paul is referencing in this verse. Christ is the head of man; it is Christ that provides man with leadership, direction, purpose, and life. Jesus said, *"I am the vine, ye are the branches: He that abideth in me, and I in him, the same bringeth forth much fruit:*

for without me ye can do nothing" (John 15:5). Christ leads
and provides so that man is able to bear fruit for God.
Man does not lead Christ, but it is Christ that leads
man. In the same way, we are told that *"the head of the
woman is the man."* This concept falls directly in line with
Eve's creation, as discussed above. Man is ordained to
be the head of the family. He is to provide the direction
and leadership for the wife and the family in the same
manner in which he is provided as much by Christ. It
is all too common today for women to grab the reins of
the family and just as common for men to allow them
to do so. God has called for the woman to be a helper
for the man and to be under his headship, and not the
other way around. It is sin to do otherwise. "But that's
not fair! Too many women are much more qualified to
lead their families than their husbands are. They are often smarter, more disciplined, and have more common
sense. How can this be what is best for any family in
this situation?" God always expects us to hear His word,
then believe His word, then obey His word. The wise
wife will spend many hours over her married life praying for her husband; she prays for his guidance, for his
wisdom, for his leadership, for his discernment, and
for so many other things. God sees everything, and He
will honor the prayers of a faithful wife who is committing her husband and her family into God's hands. In
the end, God will hold the husband accountable for the

decisions and consequences in the family. God will also hold the wife accountable for her faithfulness to her role as He established it. There is a proverb that states, *"Every wise woman buildeth her house: but the foolish plucketh it down with her hands" (Proverbs 14:1).* The wise woman submits to the headship of her husband, not because he is smarter or stronger or more qualified, but because God has commanded it, and by so doing, she builds her house. The foolish woman refuses the headship of her husband and, by doing so, plucks down her own house with her own hands. Sadly, this is all too common today, and the results are readily seen.

One of the miracles in this life that we see daily is the birth of children. It is truly amazing that God can fashion a new life in the womb of a woman by taking traits and characteristics from both the father and the mother. The new life is a mesh of father and mother, and with the birth of the first child, the life of the parents is radically altered. Children are a blessing from God, but they are also a tremendous responsibility that we cannot shun. To do so is to forge a hard life for them. God provides plenty of guidance when it comes to raising children. We are told to *"bring them up in the nurture and admonition of the Lord" (Ephesians 6:4).* What does this mean? It means that we are to teach them about the love of God and the teachings of God. Moses told the people,

And these words, which I command thee this day, shall be in thine heart: and thou shalt teach them diligently unto thy children, and shalt talk of them when thou sittest in thine house, and when thou walkest by the way, and when thou liest down, and when thou risest up.

Deuteronomy 6:6-7

It is clear that God expects the husband and wife to lead their children in their journey to God through His word. I can't see a better way to love a child than to lead that child to Jesus. Now I have heard numerous people over the years declare that they were not going to push "religion" on their children because that is what their parents did to them, and they didn't like it. Instead, they were going to let their children make their own choices and discoveries; they were not going to interfere or force them to go to church. I know this sounds like these parents have good intentions, but such a statement makes it very clear to me that the parents do not know God or God's word. The character of God demands that sin be dealt with, and God's word confirms that the lost sinner will be banished to a place called hell for eternity. Now that being the case, why would any parent who claims to love his or her child allow them to wander about aimlessly, hoping that some-day they might find Jesus? That is ridiculous! It would be worse than having that child bitten by a poisonous serpent with only moments to live unless he is treated with anti-venom, to wander around the hallways of a hospital with hundreds of doors desperately looking for the anti-venom behind each door, all the while the parents knowing exactly which door would lead to the cure. This is exactly the case of any believer who refuses to lead their child to Jesus through the word of God. That child is headed down the broad highway to hell with hundreds of religions available to them in the world, none of which will save them. Why would any loving parent allow that? God tells us that He expects us to lead that child to Jesus and have Bible teaching as a normal part of our family life. In my home, we did Bible studies while the children were still living under our roof. Many times, they would have friends visiting when it was time for Bible study, and their friends got to join us during those times. Today, the children are gone, but we still do Bible study two days per week by conference call. The impact of these Bible studies as a family will only be known to us when we arrive in glory. Our job is to be faithful in teaching and leading our children in the nurture and admonition of the Lord.

As part of teaching and leading a child, parents must impose rules and discipline in the child's life. The child will eventually learn that society has rules and consequences for breaking those rules. Isn't it better they learn those lessons at home before they step out into society and learn the hard way? Solomon provided great wisdom and direction for raising our children in this regard. He said, *"Train up a child in the way he should go: and when he is old, he will not depart from it"* (Proverbs 22:6). Here we see that if we train the child and lead him appropriately as God has instructed by teaching them the word of God, the child will remain on that godly path when he is older. A more loving act a parent cannot perform for the child.

"But what about discipline? How should that be done?" Before we get into that, when should discipline begin? Solomon said, *"Chasten thy son while there is hope, and let not thy soul spare for his crying"* (Proverbs 19:18). When I was a teenager, my father told me that if I ever became a father one day, I needed to love and train my children when they were young. He said if I didn't do that, they would never be close to me or respect me. He then gave me an illustration that I have never forgotten. He reminded me that when a new calf is born (I was raised in cattle country in deep south Texas), if I take that calf right after it is born, and I hold it, caress it, feed it from a bottle, and love on it, then that calf will always follow me even into adulthood. It will let me hug it, pet it, and feed it by hand. But if that same calf is born, and I wait two weeks to begin trying to hold it and feed it, he said, "I will never get close to that animal. It will drag me around and avoid me its whole life." He went on to say that children are exactly the same. If you take them early and teach them and love them and discipline them, they will love and respect you their whole lives. But if you wait until they are older to get involved with them, they will rebel and never be close to you. In this proverb, Solomon is telling us to get involved in our children's lives early ("while there is hope"). We should start working with our children immediately; reading to them, singing to them, talking to them, and holding them. They should begin to recognize our voice and our smell, and it should be a comfort to them.

As the children grow, we are called to provide guidance and discipline. The discipline is to be imposed, even when the child is crying, as Solomon notes above. This reminds me of when I would spank my oldest; she would start screaming and crying even before I had spanked her. With many parents, this tactic would have prevented them from imposing the spanking. "After all, she is already suffering enough," Solomon says not to be taken in by that logic. Impose the punishment, *"and let not thy soul spare for his crying."* Children (and some adults, too) are filled with youthful ideas that are sinful and that lead them down errant paths. Solomon said that discipline corrects those when he said, *"Foolishness is bound in the heart of a child: but the rod of correction shall drive it far from him" (Proverbs 22:15).* Solomon envisioned corporeal punishment, the physical discipline of the child. However, spanking is to be exercised in love, not in anger. Never spank a child while angry. It is better to wait until you have cooled down, then you can come back, impose the punishment, and explain to the child afterward why it was necessary. This is how the child learns, and he will respect and love you for it (especially when he becomes an adult).

Children are called to honor their parents and to be obedient to them. The fifth commandment that God gave Moses states, *"Honour thy father and thy mother: that thy days may be long upon the land which the LORD thy God giveth thee" (Exodus 20:12).* Notice what is not here; God does not set a time limit on this commandment. Many people believe that once they become adults, this commandment ends. That is not true. We are always to give honor and respect to our parents so long as they live, and our age does not make a difference. The Bible also requires children to obey their parents. *"Children, obey your parents in the Lord: for this is right" (Ephesians 6:1).* Notice that in the Moses passage in Exodus 20, the commandment is not directed towards children. That passage was directed towards all the Jewish people, old and young. This *Ephesians* passage is directed to "children." While a person is still a child, that child is to obey his or her parents, "for this is right." Once the child becomes an adult and moves away, the child is to continue to honor the parents but is free from having to obey (although I would expect that most of the time that would not be a problem).To have a family is a tremendous gift from God, but to have that family flourish requires a tremendous responsibility and commitment from all family members. It starts with the husband who leads the family in strength and love. It continues with the wife who supports the husband in this task. And it ends with the children who are taught of their parents and who reciprocate love, affection, and respect back to them.

CHAPTER 14

How Should We Live in Light of Our Government?

When I turned on the television yesterday (late summer, 2020), there was mass chaos happening in several of our cities. Looting, rioting, and violence were brought into my home through digital media. For others, this extremism was brought into their homes quite literally. Police officers and other governmental personnel arrived on the scene, but little was done to effectively stop the onslaught. The mob would not hear or obey the commands from authorities to disperse and stand down. Instead, it intensified its efforts by hurling projectiles at law enforcement, shining lasers at their eyes, burning private property, and even committing murder. It was a tragic sight to behold for anyone who loves this country. Without knowing any of the people participating in the mob activities, I am quite confident that many of the participants felt justified in their methods. After all, the underlying cause(s) which drove these individuals must have been important enough in their minds to defy the governmental authorities. But is this type of defiance permitted in the sight of God?

Paul wrote, *"Let every soul be subject unto the higher powers. For there is no power but of God: the powers that be are ordained of God" (Romans 13:1).* The "higher powers" in this passage is the government, and you will notice that they exist because of God since He ordained them. In other words, all government exists because God created it, and the people are to "be subject unto the higher powers." God's people are to be obedient to the government under which they live. Let's look at the entire passage.

> Let every soul be subject unto the higher powers. For there is no power but of God: the powers that be are ordained of God. Whosoever therefore resisteth the power, resisteth the ordinance of God: and they that resist shall receive to themselves damnation. For rulers are not a terror to good works, but to the evil. Wilt thou then not be afraid of the power? do that which is good, and thou shalt have praise of the same: For he is the minister of God to thee for good. But if thou do that which is

evil, be afraid; for he beareth not the sword in vain: for he is the minister of God, a revenger to execute wrath upon him that doeth evil. Wherefore ye must needs be subject, not only for wrath, but also for conscience sake.

Romans 13:1-5

So we can see from this passage that if we resist our government, we resist the law of God. God equates the two. "But how can this be? Our governments are corrupt, and many of their laws are too." We'll address this matter later in the chapter. For now, God sees rebellion against the government the same as rebellion against God Himself. But why? God knows that without government, given the sinful nature of man, society would digress into lawlessness, much like the rioting I saw on television yesterday. Only this lawlessness wouldn't be a thing that occurs on rare occasions as in our society; it would be a regular part of our lives since there would be no check or consequence to behavior that today would be considered aggressive or unlawful. Without law, the strong would take whatever they want, and the weak would have no remedy. This would lead to a society devoid of peace and the assurance of tomorrow's security.

If we look further into the passage above, we see another reason we are commanded to submit to the government: *"For rulers are not a terror to good works, but to the evil...For he is the minister of God to thee for good."* This passage reveals something very interesting. It assumes that the government is not corrupt but submits itself to the rules and laws of God. The "rulers" in our passage above are the government officials, and it states that they don't seek to be trouble to those doing good, only to those doing evil. Then it goes on to state that the government *"is the minister of God to thee for good."* Imagine that; our government, ministering to its citizens on God's behalf! What a novel idea! As such, it is clearly presumed in this passage that the government is run pursuant to the laws of God. Now we all know that in our world, a government is typically an entity, not a living person. The governmental entity is comprised of government officials, most of whom are elected. So here is a serious question for you to consider: How can God's plan for government properly function and be God's minister in society when only the ungodly run for office? For too long, Christians have stood on the sidelines watching and complaining about the corrupt officials high in our governments, all the while never considering running for office themselves; some of them never even voting. God's plan envisions godly people serving in government so that government can have its proper role in our society. It is the duty of every believer to be involved in all our elections so that the candidates who are devoted believers are supported. If all God's people participated in each election and voted for the candidate whose principles align with God's word, God's candidate would win by a landslide, and government would begin operating according to God's plan. What a difference we would see! Today, too many politicians have taken hold of power and refuse to give it up; service in government is not about the people who elected them; it's about getting wealthy and more powerful and usually at the expense of the people. It's tragic. The decisions of our government directly impact many aspects of our daily lives. Shouldn't those decisions be made with God's principles in mind instead of the personal agendas of the politicians?

We are told in scripture to pray for our governmental leaders.

> I exhort therefore, that, first of all, supplications, prayers, intercessions, and giving of thanks be made for all men; for kings, and for all that are in authority; that we may lead a quiet and peaceable life in all godliness and honesty. For this is good and acceptable in the sight of God our Savior.
>
> *1 Timothy 2:1-3*

In sharp contrast to many in our society today, including the media, the child of God is instructed to pray for our leaders in government. We are not to berate them, attack them, or demonize them, which is the norm in our world today. God has called us to support His government, and there is no better way to do so than to obey the rule of law and pray. Notice the reason we are called to pray for our leaders: *"that we may lead a quiet and peaceable life in all godliness and honesty."* God knows that the decisions of government can have a drastic impact on the lives we lead in our homes. As such, He calls for us to pray for our leaders so that the decisions they make will allow us to live peaceably and with godliness. In the 1920s and the early 1930s, the German people were reeling from the loss of World War I. German pride had taken a huge blow, and its people were bearing the burden of the monetary reparations the government was forced to pay to the victorious nations. People had lost their life savings due to hyperinflation, and the future looked bleak. They didn't think things could get any worse. Then, a fast-talking hardliner sought to restore Germany's pride through hatred, violence, and blame. He led violent protests and rallies, and his followers were all too eager to support him by any means necessary. Because the German people were desperate for somebody to lead them out of their dark state, in 1932, they voted this man into power, and on January 1, 1933, Adolf Hitler took his place in the German government. This one man soon found himself in the position of absolute power, answering to no one. He did as he pleased, and anybody that opposed him usually ended up dead or imprisoned. Because of his ideas and policies, soon, the entire German nation found themselves engulfed in a new war. Fathers and sons were taken from their homes to fight for Germany; German cities were no longer safe as bombs would soon be falling from the skies in their streets; food became scarce, and families were starving; many families moved to underground shelters as protection from the bombs and resulting fires; others found that they could no longer voice any criticisms of Hitler or the government's policies for fear of arrest by the Gestapo. The entire fabric of the life of the German people was radically altered for the worse because of the man who they elected to a high position in their government. Nobody in the German society was living in peace. The government was not functioning as the minister of God as it was designed. Instead, it was operating as the personal treasury and attack dog of Hitler. Elections have consequences, and often those consequences can be very painful.

God's command to us is that we pray for these individuals in power so we can live in peace. But the verse also says we should pray for our leaders so that we can lead lives "in all godliness and honesty." So, in addition to being at peace in our homes and daily lives, we should pray for our leaders so we can live godly lives. The decisions of government can also lead to more godly living or too rebellious living, and we pray so our officials make the right decisions for us. When the United States was founded and our Constitution along with the Bill of Rights enacted, Congress itself printed Bibles that were used as the first textbooks in our classrooms. I bet you didn't know that! The founding fathers who wrote the First Amendment that today is often cited by judges as the reason for separating church and state are the very same persons who, through Congress, printed Bibles to be used by the public. Children were taught to read and write using God's word. This decision drew people closer to God, implanting His word in the hearts of the children at that time, ultimately creating a more harmonious society. Two hundred years later, and our same government has kicked God out of our schools and public life, making it much harder to live peaceful lives in godliness. There can be no peace when laws are passed by our government that put us in direct conflict with God's word. So what are we to do when that happens, and our government has become corrupt?

We saw from the passage in *Romans 13* above that God has called us to submit to the government and not to rebel and that rebellion against the government is the same as rebellion against God. We also saw that the passage stated that the government is God's creation and is to be God's minister in society. But when the ungodly are the ones serving as our government officials, it is to be expected that ungodly decisions will come forth from our halls of government. So are we to support such ungodly laws as abortion, same-sex marriages? (I can hear some people huffing. "Who says these are 'ungodly' laws?" This book is not designed to deal with this issue in any kind of detail since we are handling only fundamental Bible doctrines. Suffice it to say that the Bible is unequivocally clear on both of these two subjects, and I must remain true to the Bible.) Let's look at two examples within the Bible that should provide our answer.

In *Exodus 1*, a new Pharaoh took command of Egypt, and he was concerned about the large Jewish population within his borders. He decided on a course of action to deal with the problem that was dark and demonic. He commanded that the midwives who were helping in the birth process of the Jews were to kill the newborn if it was a boy. By doing this, Pharaoh would eventually kill off the Jewish race. This was the royal decree, and it was given directly to the midwives. However, the midwives refused to obey. But in order to save their own necks, when Pharaoh called them in to explain why they disobeyed (because Pharaoh surely would have had them executed for their rebellion), they lied to him, saying that the Jewish mothers gave birth too fast so that the midwives could not get there in time to carry out the order. Then the Bible says, *"Therefore God dealt well with the midwives: and the people multiplied, and waxed very mighty. And it came to pass, because the midwives feared God, that he made them houses" (Exodus 1:20-21)*. So we can see that when Pharaoh's command was contrary to God's word ("thou shalt not kill"), God approved of the refusal to obey and blessed the "rebels" for it. About nine hundred years later, in *Daniel 6*, a decree was made by king Darius that for thirty days, nobody could pray to any god except for prayers made directly to Darius himself, who was clearly a man. At the time of the decree, Daniel was the second in command of the entire empire. Daniel had not been aware of the decree being made until it was already the law. Prior to the issuance of this decree, Daniel had a custom of praying three times per day towards Jerusalem. After the royal edict, Daniel kept right on praying! In fact, he even opened up his windows to the east so that anybody passing by could see him praying. You know the rest of the story. Daniel is reported to the king for his rebellion, and the king is forced to cast him into a den of hungry lions. God shut the lions' mouths, and they did no harm to Daniel. Again, God protected and blessed Daniel for his rebellion since the law was contrary to God's word (*"I am the LORD thy God...Thou shalt have no other gods before me"*). So the principle of God's word is that if a law of government is clearly contrary to God's word, we are called to rebel against the law. Otherwise, we are to submit. One other thing to consider: the "rebellion" of Daniel and the midwives was not violent; it was peaceful but firm. God's people should not be the instigators of violence as a means of godly rebellion.

But how should we pray for our governmental leaders? We should pray for their wisdom, that they would have insight and understanding as to how the decisions they make will impact the people they govern. We should pray for their salvation, that they would come to believe that God's word is supreme, that their decisions would be in conformity with the commandments and precepts of God as laid out in the Bible. We should pray for their guidance and that God would surround them with wise and godly counselors. "You have to be kidding, right? These politicians are all about themselves. They don't care about us." That may be true, but our job is to be obedient to what God has said. Do you believe there is anybody who is beyond the reach of God? Anybody who is just too mean, wicked, nasty, or rebellious that God can't save him or her? God asked a similar question:

> Is my hand shortened at all, that it cannot redeem? or have I no power to deliver? behold, at my rebuke I dry up the sea, I make the riv-

ers a wilderness: their fish stinketh, because there is no water, and dieth for thirst.

Isaiah 50:2

Later, He provides the answer to His own question: *"Behold, the LORD's hand is not shortened, that it cannot save; neither his ear heavy, that it cannot hear"* (Isaiah 59:1). In other words, nobody is beyond the reach of God, including our most corrupt government officials. Nobody knows whether our prayers may lead to the ultimate salvation and conversion of their souls.

God rules in the kingdom of men; He sets up kings, and He takes them down. Approximately two thousand six hundred years ago, the most powerful man in the whole world was a man named Nebuchadnezzar, who was the king of the Babylonian empire. It was the world superpower at the time, and Nebuchadnezzar did whatever his heart desired. He would kill entire families if he so felt, and he answered to absolutely nobody. History records that he was brutal and prone to sharp mood swings, often flying into a rage. It was not uncommon for death to be carried out for little to no reason at all. (See *Daniel 2* and *3* for examples.) Yet, one night while this king was sleeping at the height of his power, God sent a dream to him. The dream was strange, and it shook the king to his core. He was immediately awake and sought to understand the dream.

Daniel eventually provided the interpretation for the king, which involved God's judgment against the king for his pride and failure to give honor to God for all of his accomplishments. Daniel told the king as part of his interpretation that the judgment forewarned in the dream was decreed by God. He said,

> This matter is by the decree of the watchers, and the demand by the word of the holy ones: to the intent that the living may know that the most High ruleth in the kingdom of men, and giveth it to whomsoever he will, and setteth up over it the basest of men.
>
> *Daniel 4:17*

Here we are told that God rules in the kingdom of men (our governments), and He sets up whomsoever He wishes to serve in those positions. That is still true today. "But that is crazy! These politicians are so corrupt and ungodly. How can this be that God would put *them* in office?" The verse above says that God puts in office even "the basest of men." God has His reasons, and while I, personally, do not like our crooked officials, God can still use them for His purposes. Because it is clear that God still rules in the kingdom of men, we can rest assured that the decisions they make are not a surprise to God. Our hope is that those decisions will allow us to lead peaceful lives. By the way, God saved and transformed that horrible king, Nebuchadnezzar, so I know He can save and transform anybody! So don't fret when you don't like the results of an election. God controls it all. Still, since we are *not* God, we must get involved in the governmental election process to support and encourage godly candidates. Only then can government truly function as God planned it.

CHAPTER 15

Heaven and Hell: Real Places or Just Imaginary Concepts?

While growing up in the ranch country that is South Texas, where the Mexican American population and its culture were dominant, several stories were told of strange and terrifying monsters and boogeymen that would come to claim children who behaved badly. The prominent one was El Cucuy. He is said to have glowing red eyes and hides in children's bedrooms to steal them away when they misbehave. I have come to learn that many countries have similar stories. For a young mind, these stories were quite disturbing, thinking that as a result of an episode of bad behavior, I might have ended up an unwilling victim in the clutches of an evil being. But was El Cucuy real or just an imaginary concept designed to get children to obey? As an adult today, I am confident this was an imaginary concept and not something real.

Is the same true of the doctrine of heaven and hell, the place where the saved live in eternal bliss with God and the place where the lost live in eternal torment with the devil? Are these places real, or are they imaginary concepts designed to get people to live in accordance with God's principles? Few doctrines in religious circles draw a sharper, more heated debate than the doctrine of the existence of a real heaven or a real hell. Can there really be an eternal consequence for a human soul after death based upon a person's choice in this life? The Bible is clear on this: there is absolutely a real heaven and a real hell.

Heaven

It might surprise you to know that the Bible teaches that there are three heavens. Two of these heavens, however, might not be what you expect. The first heaven is found in *Genesis 1*, where we read,

> And God made the firmament, and divided the waters which were under the firmament from the waters which were above the firmament: and it was so. And God called the firmament Heaven. And the evening and the morning were the second day.
>
> *Genesis 1:7-8*

The "firmament" is our atmosphere, and it is the first heaven. You can see this confirmed later in the chapter when Moses writes, *"And God said, Let the waters bring forth abundantly the moving creature that hath life, and fowl that may fly above the earth in the open firmament of heaven"* (Genesis 1:20). The second heaven is also found in the same chapter of Genesis. Here we read:

> And God said, Let there be lights in the firmament of the heaven to divide the day from the night; and let them be for signs, and for seasons, and for days, and years: And let them be for lights in the firmament of the heaven to give light upon the earth: and it was so. And God made two great lights; the greater light to rule the day, and the lesser light to rule the night: he made the stars also. And God set them in the firmament of the heaven to give light upon the earth.
>
> *Genesis 1:14-17*

So we can clearly see that this second heaven is the place where God put the sun, moon, and stars. We call this outer space, and it is the second heaven. However, it is the third heaven that will draw the focus of our discussion.

Paul the apostle wrote,

> I knew a man in Christ above fourteen years ago, (whether in the body, I cannot tell; or whether out of the body, I cannot tell: God knoweth;) such an one caught up to the third heaven...How that he was caught up into paradise, and heard unspeakable words, which it is not lawful for a man to utter.
>
> *2 Corinthians 12:2, 4*

Paul says this man (he was speaking about himself in this passage) was lifted up into the third heaven, which he described as paradise. So vivid was this event that Paul could not tell whether it was a vision he saw or whether he was really there for that moment in time. Yet what is clear is that Paul was transported to a place where he saw and heard things that were clear and definitive. "Wait a minute!" you say. "Who is to say that he didn't simply have a vivid dream which he confused for a real visit, whether in the body or not? You surely can't be so certain that there is a real heaven based on just this passage. Paul himself can't say whether he was there in person or not, so how can you be so sure?" Well, nothing in the passage indicates that Paul dreamed all of this. In fact, if you read verse 1 of chapter 12, you will find that Paul says that if he was to brag about himself, he would come to "visions and revelations" of the Lord.

Then he describes the third heaven. Still, there are many other things to consider, so please be patient.

God Himself claims to rule from heaven. *"The LORD is in his holy temple, the LORD's throne is in heaven: his eyes behold, his eyelids try, the children of men" (Psalm 11:4)*. Here we can see that God's throne and temple are in heaven. Isaiah said the same thing when he wrote, *"Thus saith the LORD, The heaven is my throne, and the earth is my footstool: where is the house that ye build unto me? and where is the place of my rest?" (Isaiah 66:1)* Jesus Himself, when teaching His disciples to pray, said, *"After this manner therefore pray ye: Our Father which art in heaven, Hallowed be thy name" (Matthew 6:9)*. Jesus said that God the Father was in heaven. Jesus also said, *"But I say unto you, Swear not at all; neither by heaven; for it is God's throne: Nor by the earth; for it is his footstool" (Matthew 5:34-35)*. Many times Jesus spoke of God as His Father. God was not imaginary but real, and this real God resides in a definitive, real place that Jesus and the other writers in scripture call heaven.

When God created our world, He created a place called the Garden of Eden. It was here that He placed Adam and Eve. This place was a perfect paradise on earth. It was a place where crops and orchards grew themselves; a place where no weeds, thorns, or poisonous plants existed; where the animals all lived in peace with man and with each other; a place where there was no sickness, hurt, or sin; and a place with everything anybody could want or need. God created this place to be a perfect place on earth where God could commune with man without barriers. But when sin entered the Garden after the fall of Adam, this perfect place was lost, as was man's intimate communion with God. But God already had something much better in mind.

During Moses' life, God entrusted Moses with tremendous responsibility resulting in the liberation of the Jewish people from under the hand of Pharaoh. Moses was faithful in his duties, and Moses was able to speak to God face to face, something nobody else was able to do. *"And the LORD spake unto Moses face to face, as a man speaketh unto his friend" (Exodus 33:11).* (See also *Numbers 12:6-8.*) Now imagine being able to speak to God eyeball to eyeball! That must have been the ultimate experience for any person! Yet, Moses was not satisfied. He knew there was much more to God that he hadn't known or experienced. The Bible says, *"And he said, I beseech thee, shew me thy glory" (Exodus 33:18).* Moses asked God to see His full glory. Up to this point, God had spoken to Moses by appearing in human form, but God's glory was veiled so that Moses could not see it. Moses desired to see God without any barrier limiting His glory. God quickly responded by saying, *"And he said, Thou canst not see my face: for there shall no man see me, and live" (Exodus 33:20).* God said that no man could see the full glory of God and live; Moses could only see

God in a human body that masked His true glory. Moses would never see it, and neither would anybody else.

Approximately one thousand four hundred years after Moses, Jesus was born in Bethlehem, fulfilling numerous prophecies, including *Isaiah 7:14*, which said that a virgin would conceive and bear a son and his name would be called Immanuel. Immanuel means "God with us," according to *Matthew 1:23*. Jesus was God among men, yet Jesus' glory was fully masked in the human body, which God the Father fashioned for Him so that nobody saw Him in His full glory. Peter, James, and John saw a glimpse of it at the mount of transfiguration, but they would not have been able to see Jesus' full glory and live.

The point of all of this is that God knew that heaven would be better than anything that could be created on earth. In heaven, we will see God face to face, as did Moses, but this time in all His glory. Remember, all believers will appear in heaven, and we will be given new bodies that are like Jesus' glorified body. *"Beloved, now are we the sons of God, and it doth not yet appear what we shall be: but we know that, when he shall appear, we shall be like him; for we shall see him as he is"* (1 John 3:2). Notice the passage here states that we "shall be like him." We are going to receive glorified, incorruptible bodies that will be like Jesus' body. (See also *1 Corinthians 15:42-53*.) With this type of body, we "shall see him as he is," and we won't die. God has planned for His people to live with Him (*Revelation 21:3*) and see Him in His full glory for all eternity. What a gift! If this were all that heaven was, we would be most blessed. But God has prepared heaven as so much more. God will forever destroy this current earth and the heavens and will create new ones. I absolutely love the beauty of our world, from the snow-capped mountains to the lush green valleys, from the white, sandy beaches to the quiet, gentle brooks. But the new world to come will be infinitely grander and more beautiful.

In *Revelation 21* and 22, we are told of the new Jerusalem that God Himself designed and built. It is a glorious place where God will reside with His people. Many staggering details are provided about this city, including its dimensions (approximately one thousand five hundred miles long, one thousand five hundred miles wide, and one thousand five hundred miles high!) and its street materials (translucent gold). People have long tried to imagine what heaven will be like, with its beauty and wonders, but it simply cannot be done. The Bible says, *"But as it is written, Eye hath not seen, nor ear heard, neither have entered into the heart of man, the things which God hath prepared for them that love him"* (1 Corinthians 2:9). Heaven is beyond your wildest dreams, and it is very real. But this is a place for only the saved. The lost have a very different fate.

Hell

Many religious people fight and argue over the existence of a real place called hell. Hell is the lake of fire as described in *Revelation 19:20; 20:10,14*. It is said to be a place of absolute torment and pain that lasts for all eternity. But while heaven may be real, is hell? After all, heaven describes a perfect paradise where man resides with God for all eternity, and it is a blessing; this conforms to our image of a loving God. But many argue that a loving God would never cause anybody to suffer eternal pain, suffering, and torment; that, they argue, would be very cruel and against God's nature. But what "they" say doesn't matter. What does the Bible say?

No character in the Bible spoke more about hell than Jesus. Jesus said that it is a place prepared for the devil and his angels. *"Then shall he say also unto them on the left hand, Depart from me, ye cursed, into everlasting fire, prepared for the devil and his angels" (Matthew 25:41).* Notice first of all that these lost souls are commanded to depart "into everlasting fire." This is a specific place where these souls will be banished. "I don't believe that," you say. "It could just as easily mean that these lost souls are destroyed or annihilated, as symbolized by the fire." If a soul is destroyed so that it no longer exists, then the result is a condition of the soul. Jesus said these were to depart to a place. But hold on; there is more we will get to shortly.

Notice also in this verse that Jesus says that the everlasting fire "was prepared"; this speaks of something that was created for a purpose, and that purpose is revealed in the last portion of this verse: it was created for the devil and his angels. Because of the rebellion of Satan and the angelic host who rejected God and joined the rebellion, the punishment is banishment in this lake of fire. There is no hope of salvation for these. Jesus did not die for lost angels; He only died for lost man.

The other thing to notice here is that the fire is "everlasting." This means the fire never goes out; it is eternal. "Well, who cares if it's eternal? Nobody lives forever anyway," you may be saying. But Jesus said,

> And if thy hand offend thee, cut it off: it is better for thee to enter into life maimed, than having two hands to go into hell, into the fire that never shall be quenched: where their worm dieth not, and the fire is not quenched.
>
> *Mark 9:43-44*

Notice that "their worm" doesn't die. This refers to the souls of the lost; they will not die in this eternal fire. Whether or not you know it, all souls are eternal. The only question is where that soul will live after this life ends. "But that is outrageous! It's unloving and unkind. Its cruel and unusual punishment to the extreme, and it is totally against the loving nature of God. Surely you can't be right!" Isaiah spoke of the "strange work" of

God, when he said, *"For the LORD shall rise up as in mount Perazim, he shall be wroth as in the valley of Gibeon, that he may do his work, his strange work; and bring to pass his act, his strange act"* (Isaiah 28:21). And what is this strange work? It is the judgment of the lost souls of men and the pronouncement of their eternal fate in the lake of fire. This can be seen in *Revelation 20:11-15:*

And I saw a great white throne, and him that sat on it, from whose face the earth and the heaven fled away; and there was found no place for them. And I saw the dead [the lost], small and great, stand before God; and the books were opened: and another book was opened, which is the book of life: and the dead were judged out of those things which were written in the books, according to their works. And the sea gave up the dead which were in it; and death and hell [the grave] delivered up the dead which were in them: and they were judged every man according to their works. And death and hell were cast into the lake of fire. This is the second death. And whosoever was not found written in the book of life was cast into the lake of fire.

Revelation 20:11-15
(brackets added for clarity)

Here we find the strange work of God. "But this doesn't prove that these souls are not simply destroyed. You haven't proven anything!" you say. But the Bible teaches that they aren't destroyed. The Bible clearly teaches they are in eternal torment. Here are a few references. When Jesus returns at Armageddon to set up His kingdom, He encounters the forces of the Antichrist, his false prophet, and the armies of the world which stand against Him. In the end, the Antichrist and the false prophet are captured. Then the Bible says, *"These both were cast alive into a lake of fire burning with brimstone" (Revelation 19:20)*. If the lake of fire is simply permanent destruction, then the wording is strange. These are both cast "alive" into permanent destruction, as you suggest? That makes no sense. According to the timeline in the Bible, one thousand years later, the devil himself is cast into the lake. The Bible declares, *"And the devil that deceived them was cast into the lake of fire and brimstone, where the beast [Antichrist] and the false prophet are, and shall be tormented day and night for ever and ever" (Revelation 20:10) (brackets added for clarity)*. Notice two things here: first, it is one thousand years later, and the Antichrist and false prophet are still there; they haven't ceased to exist; and second, these are tormented without any relief forever. Can it get any clearer than that? "Well," you say, "maybe God is going to have these devils tormented, but surely not man." The Antichrist and the false prophet are not demons; they are humans led and empowered by the devil. But there is more.

During the seven-year tribulation period that is to come on this earth, the Antichrist is the head of the world government with dictatorial authority over all nations and peoples. He will implement a mark that will be required to participate in society, and without the mark, it will be impossible to live lawfully. (See *Revelation 13:16-18*.) God sends forth an angel to warn the inhabitants of the earth not to take this mark.

> And the third angel followed them, saying with a loud voice, If any man worship the beast and his image, and receive his mark in his forehead, or in his hand, the same shall drink of the wine of the wrath of God, which is poured out without mixture into the cup of his indignation; and he shall be tormented with fire and brimstone in the presence of the holy angels, and in the presence of the Lamb: and the smoke of their torment ascendeth up for ever and ever: and they have no rest day nor night, who worship the beast and his image, and whosoever received the mark of his name.
>
> *Revelation 14:9-11*

Did you see? This is a warning to humans living at the time. If they worship the Antichrist or his image or receive the mark, they are doomed to be "tormented with fire and brimstone" and "have no rest day nor night," with "the smoke of their torment ascending up for ever and ever." These are not demons but lost human souls. You can't be destroyed and still have no rest; you can't be destroyed and still be tormented. When Jesus described hell, He said it was a place of "outer darkness" where "there shall be weeping and gnashing of teeth" (*Matthew 8:12; 22:13; 25:30*). Hell is a place where there is no light, even though there is fire. It is also a place of weeping and gnashing of teeth. Now I have a question for you. If hell is the destruction or annihilation of the lost soul, then how can there be any consciousness? Jesus said that in hell, there will be weeping. Weeping is what we do when we are in pain, either physically or emotionally. We cry when the pain is too intense, or we are in deep misery. There is also gnashing of teeth. This occurs when we are in bitter frustration. This is exactly the state of all the lost who will be in hell. But why? We'll get to that in just a moment—one more thing to look at first.

In *Luke 16:19-31*, Jesus speaks a fascinating parable about a rich man and a poor man. The rich man lives for himself and takes no interest in those around him. When the rich man died, Jesus said:

the rich man also died, and was buried; and in hell he lift up his eyes, being in torments, and seeth Abraham afar off, and Lazarus [the poor man] in his bosom. And he [the rich man] cried and said, Father Abraham, have mercy on me, and send Lazarus, that he may dip the tip of his finger in water, and cool my tongue; for I am tormented in this flame.

Luke 16:22-24 (brackets added for clarity)

Here we can see that Jesus clearly taught that after the man was buried, being lost, he was in torment in the flames, and he cannot find relief. This is the reason for the weeping and the gnashing of the teeth that Jesus spoke about.

Why would God create such a horrible place and allow the lost to suffer there eternally? Simply put, hell is designed to be a place where God is not present. Since the lost refused to humble themselves and come to Jesus for salvation and insisted on living life without God, they get to live in a place where God will not be present. Let me explain. Hell is described as a place of intense darkness. Why? Because God is light! *"This then is the message which we have heard of him, and declare unto you, that God is light, and in him is no darkness at all"* (1 John 1:5). Hell is intense darkness because God is not there. Hell is a place of sorrow because no soul can find joy apart from Jesus, and Jesus is not there. The human soul was designed to find its joy and peace in God, and without God, there can be no joy and no peace. This is why it is a place of suffering and torment. Hell is a place of fire because fire always speaks of judgment, and since the lost never came to Jesus for salvation, judgment is what justice demands. In the end, every lost soul will go through the second death (which we saw above), which is eternal separation from God. This separation ends with a final destination in the lake of fire where the lost never find relief from the torment.

God said, *"I have long time holden my peace; I have been still, and refrained myself; now will I cry like a travailing woman; I will destroy and devour at once"* (Isaiah 42:14). Today, God is holding His peace and has not yet moved in judgment. The fact that you are reading this book proves that you still have hope. It is still not too late to come to Jesus and be saved. Put your trust in Him today. There is no reason you have to suffer the fate of the lost in the very real place called hell.

Do You Want to Be Saved? Here's How

Are you being convicted by the Holy Spirit that you need to be saved? With God, the transaction is quite simple, and it all centers on faith in the finished work of Jesus Christ. Before we look at this simple transaction according to the Bible, I think it is important to review some Jewish history. Turn your gaze to Egypt about one thousand four hundred years before the birth of Jesus.

Can you see it? The landscape is barren. The people are scared and nervous, and there is a sense of fear in the air. The country has endured nine plagues from the God of Moses, each one coming to pass just as Moses had said. First, the great Nile river, which is the lifeline of the country, was turned into a flowing river of blood. Dead fish floated along the crimson currents for seven days, and it stank horribly. After Pharaoh refused to release the Jews, more judgments came. Frogs filled up the landscape, as did lice and hoards of locusts. They soiled the food supply and stripped the landscape bare. Food became scarce. To make things worse, great hailstones fell from the sky, damaging much of the trees and other food-bearing plants, as well as killing much livestock. And still, it got worse. Now, Moses has just made another prediction, his boldest one yet. He said that God will send the destroyer into Egypt this very night and will destroy all the firstborn in Egypt, from the firstborn of Pharaoh to those of the animals. Everybody is very worried as nightfall approaches.

But Moses called the elders of the Jews and told them what God was going to do that night. Moses went on to explain that the destroyer would kill all the firstborn in the land of Egypt except for those that followed Moses' instructions. Moses told them to kill the Passover lamb and save its blood in a basin. The people were then to take of that blood and paint it upon the doorposts of the house. Then remain inside the house all night. Moses continued,

> For the LORD will pass through to smite the Egyptians; and when he seeth the blood upon the lintel, and on the two side posts, the LORD will pass over the door, and will not suffer the destroyer to come in unto your houses to smite you.
>
> *Exodus 12:23*

Now the people who heard Moses' instructions had a choice: they could either believe what Moses said and do exactly as he said, or they could not. Some people surely must have said, "Why on earth would I put blood on my doorposts? That stuff is going to smell and attract flies. There is no way this can be right. I'm not going to bother with that. I'm sure things will be exactly the same tomorrow as they were today." God always operates this way: believe His word and live or fail to do so and face the ultimate consequences.

The Bible records that God sent the destroyer who did exactly as Moses said.

> And it came to pass, that at midnight the LORD smote all the firstborn in the land of Egypt, from the firstborn of Pharaoh that sat on his throne unto the firstborn of the captive that was in the dungeon; and all the firstborn of cattle.
>
> *Exodus 12:29*

After this, Pharaoh let the people go.

Please consider what you have just seen. God's only requirement for the destroyer to pass them by was that the blood had to be painted on the doorposts of the house. The blood was the absolute requirement. Notice that Moses did not say, "If God finds you praying in the house" or "If God finds that you were good before this night" or "If God finds that you were a regular at church" or any other such thing. God specifically said, "when I see the blood, I will pass over you." This is the important thing, and it is exactly true today as well. We are all facing the destroyer at the end of our lives, and we are all doomed unless God sees the blood. "What blood?" you may be asking. God is looking for Jesus' blood which He spilled on the cross two thousand years ago, painted across your heart. When God sees Jesus' blood on your heart, you are free from God's wrath. That is the only requirement! Read on to see how to apply Jesus' blood to your heart today and be saved.

First, we must recognize and admit our current sinful state before God. God looks upon man and sees a rebellious sinner in need of a Savior. But you may be thinking, "I'm not a bad person. I'm really pretty nice. I am kind to other people. I don't cheat or lie, and I am faithful to my religion." This may all be true, but compared with God's standard of perfection, you (and me) fall far short. The Bible says, *"If we say that we have no sin, we deceive ourselves, and the truth is not in us"* (1 John 1:8). It also says, *"But we are all as an unclean thing and all our righteousnesses are as filthy rags; and we all do fade as a leaf; and our iniquities, like the wind, have taken us away"* (Isaiah 64:6). While there are numerous other passages that make this point, here is one more: *"For all have sinned, and come short of the glory of God"* (Romans 3:23). So the first thing we must do is humble ourselves before God and acknowledge our sin. We must admit our sins and confess them to God. Heartfelt repentance is the key. True repentance is coming to the point we agree with God that our thoughts, actions, and words have been in rebellion against God's word and a stench in the nostrils of God. This is what Jesus was referring to when He said, *"Blessed are they that mourn: for they shall be comforted" (Matthew 5:4)*. These are people who mourn over their sin in true repentance. Now after true repentance and confession of your sins, you are ready to take the next step.

Next, you must come before God and confess that without Jesus' blood shed on the cross, nobody can be saved. Tell God that you believe Jesus' death on the cross was sufficient to save you from your sins. The Bible says that through Jesus, *"we have redemption through his blood, the forgiveness of sins, according to the riches of his grace" (Ephesians 1:7)*. It also says,

> But God commendeth [proves] his love toward us, in that, while we were yet sinners, Christ died for us. Much more then, being now justified by his blood, we shall be saved from wrath through him.
> *Romans 5:8-9* (brackets added for clarity)

You can see from these two passages alone that the salvation of a human soul is totally dependent on Jesus' death on the cross. There is not a single thing you can do to add to it. *"For by grace are ye saved through faith; and that not of yourselves: it is the gift of God: not of works, lest any man should boast"* (Ephesians 2:8-9). Once you come to believe from the heart that there is nothing you can do to add to the work of Jesus, and His work alone was sufficient to wipe away your sin, you're ready to move forward. *"For with the heart man believeth unto righteousness; and with the mouth confession is made unto salvation"* (Romans 10:10).

Now, just cry out to God to save you! The Bible says: *"That if thou shalt confess with they mouth the Lord Jesus, and shalt believe in thine heart that God hath raised him from the dead, thou shalt be saved"* (Romans 10:9). Jesus said, *"For God so loved the world, that he gave his only begotten Son, that whosoever believeth in him should not perish, but have everlasting life"* (John 3:16). I urge you to please humble yourself before God in prayer and believe. Tell Him all of these things, ask Him to be your God and Savior, and you will be saved! If you have done this with all your heart, the blood of Jesus is now painted on your heart, and God sees the blood! You're saved!

This transaction is totally free to you and me; it doesn't cost us anything. However, while it may be free to you and me, it cost God everything in the death of Jesus. What love God has demonstrated for us! Do not neglect this great salvation, for judgment will come without mercy to those who do. (See *Hebrews 10:28-29*.)

About the Author

Tomas "Tommy" Ramirez III is a successful trial lawyer and Justice of the Peace in Medina County, Texas, bordering San Antonio's Bexar County. Prior to entering the field of law back in 1993, he was an engineer for Mobil Oil in Midland, Texas, where he achieved good success and earned a reputation for aggressive, forward thinking.

Ramirez was born in Kingsville, Texas, and was raised in a predominantly Catholic region. His mother made sure that church was a mandate every week, although there was very little Bible study either in church or at home. Ramirez was an inquisitive child, and he had many questions about God throughout his childhood, which his mother could not adequately answer. Ultimately, at approximately thirty years of age, Ramirez began a comprehensive study of the Holy Bible in order to know the truth about God. Since that time, Ramirez has continued to study the Bible daily and has been a teacher and supply preacher since 1997. He was licensed as a minister by First Baptist Church of Devine in June 2001.

He married to his wife, Diana, in 1993, and they have three children, one of whom died at the age of eighteen in the Texas floods of 2015. Ramirez and his family have placed their hopes in Jesus Christ and hope to bear much fruit for God's glory while they have time to do so on this earth.

CPSIA information can be obtained
at www.ICGtesting.com
Printed in the USA
BVHW051014061021
618281BV00013B/320